Beatle!

LOOK !

THREE TOP GROUPS AGAIN

NEXT WEDNESDAY NIGHT AT HAMBLETON HALL

Page Moss, Huyton

— What a terrific line up for —
WEDNESDAY, 25th JANUARY 1961

- The Sensational Beatles
- Derry & The Seniors
- Faron & The Tempest Tornadoes

YES! You must come along early and bring your friends !

PAY AT THE DOOR **2/6 before 8 p.m. 3/- afterwards**

NOTE ! No admission after 9-30 p.m.

Beatle!

THE PETE BEST STORY

PETE BEST & PATRICK DONCASTER

PLEXUS, LONDON

Published by Plexus Publishing Limited
55a Clapham Common Southside
London SW4 9BX

Best, pete
Beatle!
1. Beatles
I. Title II. Doncaster, Patrick
786.5'0092'2 ML421.B4

ISBN 0-85965-077-4

Cover design by Phil Smee
Book design by Phil Smee
Printed and bound in Great Britain by
J W Arrowsmith, Winterstoke Road, Bristol

10 9 8 7 6 5 4 3 2

A dedication to Pat, a true friend.

I would like to dedicate this book to the memory of Pat Doncaster, who tragically passed away in March of 1984, before ever seeing the book in its final form. He was a kind, warm and wonderful gentleman, without whose help, patience and hard work this book would never have been written. All I would like to say, and I hope my words convey my innermost feelings, is . . . thank you, Pat, for everything.

ACKNOWLEDGEMENTS

I would like to extend my thanks and acknowledgements to my mother, 'Mo', for participating in interviews and supplying personal pictures and memorabilia. My two brothers, Rory and Roag, and my own personal family, Kathy, Beba and Bonita – also supplied pictures.

I would also like to thank Bill Harry of *Merseybeat*; Bob Wooler, for his article in the same publication; and *New Musical Express.* For invaluable research material I would like to acknowledge my debt to *A Cellarful of Noise* by Brian Epstein, *The Beatles* by Hunter Davies, the *Daily Mirror* and *Playboy* magazine.

The photographs in this book are mostly from my own personal collection and those of my family. For their help in researching further visual material, I would especially like to thank Dick Matthews, Jim Hughes of the Cavern Mecca, Margaret Roberts of Peter Kaye Studios, Albert Marrion and Phil Smee.

I would also like to thank David Grossman of the David Grossman Literary Agency and, of course, Patrick Doncaster, for their patience and assistance. If there is anyone I have overlooked, then may they please accept my apologies. Finally, I would like to extend my grateful thanks to all at Plexus Publishing, especially to Sandra Wake and Terry Porter, Nicky Adamson and Lisa Hardy.

Credits: *Pete Best*, 2, 8/9, 10, 12, 14/15, 21, 29, 30, 34/35, 40, 44/45, 64, 65, 78, 83, 86/87, 91, 92, 110/111, 113, 114, 116/117, 119, 121, 123, 128/129, 132, 137, 138, 140/141, 146/147, 151, 161, 176, 189, 190. *Jim Hughes of Cavern Mecca*, 8/9, 24, 134/135, 151, 152/153. *Peter Kaye*, 162, 184. *Keystone*, 18/19, 34/35, 48, 60/61, 77, 128/129, 170/171. *Dick Matthews*, 90, 91, 101, 132, 134/135, 140/141. *Pictorial Press*, 25, 60/61, 139, 140/141, 180, 184/185. *Phil Smee Collection*, 18/19, 83, 86/87, 102, 124, 170/171, 181. *Star-Club Hamburg*, 154. *Syndication International*, 142.

CONTENTS

Casbah
Promotions
PRESENT A
Big Beat Dance
ST. JOHNS HALL · SNAEFELL AVENUE
TUEBROOK LIVERPOOL
On FRIDAY, 17th FEBRUARY 1961
The BEATLES Rock Combo
GENE DAY & JANGO Beats
ADMISSION 3/6
(Doors Open 7-15 p.m.)
The Management Reserve the Right to Refuse Admission

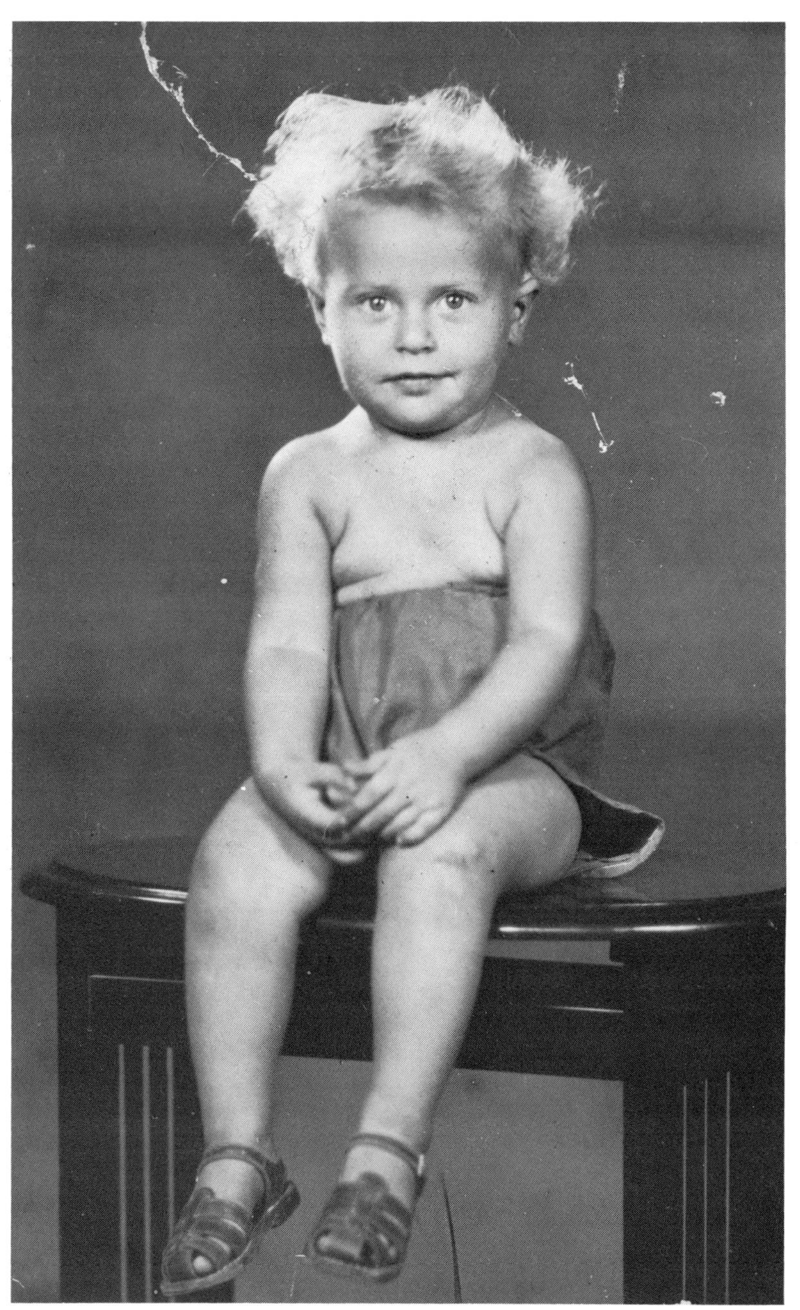

Peter, aged 21 months, in India where he spent the first four years of his life.

1

THE START OF IT ALL

Hayman's Green is a quiet suburban road in Liverpool's West Derby district, some four miles from Liverpool's bustling city centre with its hotels, department stores and pedestrian precincts. Tall trees line the road; on a summer's evening they throw long graceful shadows over the handful of peaceful bungalows and houses. Number Eight is one of the latter: a spacious, grey Victorian house with fifteen rooms. It was once my home; my mother still lives there and so does by second brother Roag, who was born in what was to be a milestone of a year – 1962.

It was at this house in Hayman's Green that I first saw three raw teenagers named John Lennon, Paul McCartney and George Harrison, who were to become my close friends and with whom I would share nearly three momentous years. When they first came into my life they were part of an amateurish group called the Quarrymen, and they were just experiencing the first uncontrollable urge to make rock'n'roll music that would eventually lead to the formation of the Beatles in 1960 – with me included. Number Eight was to become a second home for all of them, but especially for John, for it was at this house that my friendship with him began – a friendship that would last four years.

The reason that this comfortable family home was to be the focus of so many extraordinary and unpredictable events lay in the rambling cellars beneath the big old house. For it was here that the Casbah evolved, a club that began as a den for me and my other brother Rory and our school pals, but which grew into one of the favourite teenage venues in late fifties Liverpool.

My brother and I had both been born in wartime India. My father was John Best, a well known Liverpool boxing promoter – as his father had been before him. Both before and after the Second World War, Dad's bills would feature big-fight names such as Tommy Farr, Freddie Mills, Lee Savold, Floyd Paterson and the Turpin brothers, Randolph and Dick. When the war got under way he was posted to India as an Army physical training instructor and later gained his commission.

In Delhi he met and married my mother, who had been born there of English parentage and was working for the Red Cross. I was born in Madras on 24 November 1941 and given the Christian names Randolph Peter.

My mother's name is Mona; since the age of eleven or so I have called her Mo, which is short for mother as well. She soon became Mo to everybody, and still is; she is a marvellous champion of a woman who let me choose my own path in life and has supported me like a pillar whether times have been good or bad.

When the war finally ended we all sailed for Britain in the troop ship *Georgic*, arriving in Liverpool at Christmas time in 1945. Passengers included General (later Field-Marshal) Sir William Slim, the victor of Burma, with members of his 14th Army, among them the Chindits. It had been an unforgettable voyage, lashed by Force Ten gales. Brother Rory, who came along in 1944, was learning to walk and spent most of the time hanging on to me, so much so that I used to call him 'Sea-legs'.

Back home on Merseyside, Dad picked up the threads and returned to the big fight game. For the first two years we lived in the city in a flat on Casey Street, but our first real home was a new property just outside West Derby. There was one more move before we settled in Hayman's Green, where Number Eight stands back from the road behind a solid wall.

As a young boy I went to various schools until I won a scholarship to Liverpool Collegiate in Shaw Street. By my mid-teens I had chalked up five 'O' levels and had decided that perhaps the teaching profession was the one for me. I suppose you would describe us as being a middle-class family and teaching somehow seemed to fit into the pattern. That is, until the Casbah came along.

I was around sixteen when the idea began to develop. It all started out in a most casual way while I was still at school. Like most kids, I used to bring friends home and by this time we were all interested in the ever-growing world of pop music which had brought about a teenage revolution right across the world in the mid-fifties, particularly in Britain, via skiffle and rock'n'roll. Throughout the land thousands of lads were banding themselves together in groups of three or four, trying to make their own music mainly with guitars – most of them utility types – and frequently with improvised instruments such as washboards and tea-chest basses, from which a reasonable note or two could be 'slapped' from a length of string tied to a broomstick.

Among the early heroes had been the kiss-curled Bill Haley with his clowning Comets, the home-grown Lonnie Donegan and, of course, Elvis. In Liverpool we had been quick to embrace originals like Chuck Berry and Little Richard, who had been responsible for much of the fantastic onward march of rock. Besides these I liked such emerging big

The Best family. Top left: Mona ('Mo') and John Best; top right: John Best in uniform; below right: Peter and his younger brother Rory on the verandah of their Delhi bungalow; below left: the family at home in Liverpool; centre: Peter aged ten.

names as Jerry Lee Lewis, Carl Perkins and Duane Eddy; also Gene Vincent and the late Eddie Cochran, both of whom I saw on stage in Liverpool shortly before Eddie's death in a car crash in 1960, on his way to London Airport after the close of his British tour.

My friends and I would dash home from school to play records and Mo, in her wisdom, decided that the best place for a bunch of lads to create a din was in the cellar. Most homes have one cellar. Number Eight Hayman's Green was over-endowed with them – its cellar consisted of seven adjoining basement rooms. It was only natural that the cellars began to attract more and new-found friends, who saw them as a teenage haven of escape from an adult world that disapproved of rock'n'roll, preferring the staid balladeers like Perry Como and Guy Mitchell, along with Doris Day and Rosemary Clooney.

Then Mo gave birth to the big idea. Why not turn the cellars into a club? A coffee-bar type of club, like those we had read about in Soho in London, where would-be rock'n'rollers were trekking from all over the country. There were few enough places for teenagers to meet in Liverpool's centre let alone the surrounding suburbs. It seemed like a Godsend and we all responded enthusiastically.

Mo recalled those memorable days recently: 'My home was beginning to resemble a railway station at this time,' she said, 'there was always someone passing through. My original idea had been to start a little exclusive club for Peter and his friends in the cellars and thus put an end to all this trooping in and out of the living quarters. But within days the word had gone around and young people – most of them complete strangers – began to knock at my front door asking if they could join! There could never have been so much enthusiasm for a club that hadn't yet opened.'

The idea and enthusiasm would grow and grow. Eventually Mo's brainwave would result in a club with more than 2,000 members, but there would be something like six months hard labour for us all, including those friends who used to troop in and out, before we could ever think of opening the doors to the youthful public at large. There were walls to be knocked down; gallons of paint to be splashed around; a bar to be built; furnishings to be bought and a jukebox to install.

As Mo said: 'I had never done anything like this before and I had never seen the coffee bars of Soho and, of course, I never thought that the idea would snowball the way it did.

'All the labour was voluntary – all done by Peter's friends, boys and girls. There were about ten of them and they would start work after tea and would make tracks for their homes around nine-thirty. At the weekends they would stay and I fed them and supplied endless cups of tea and coffee. They were fantastic boys and girls.

'Peter's father encouraged me. "If that's what you feel you would like

Previous page: Peter and Rory in the garden of their Liverpool home. Inset top: Mona Best; left: Peter (back row, second from left) with the Liverpool Collegiate football team; right: John Best with Peter aged 14 (right) and Rory.

to do, go ahead and do it," he said at the start. He was very proud of the project as it developed.

'Never once during that exciting six months did I ever regret the immense task – as it would turn out to be – that I had taken on in deciding to make part of my home a rendezvous for young people. The enthusiasm and the happy atmosphere were wonderful.' (Some of the old volunteers, now parents themselves, still call in at Number Eight to see Mo and chat about those days.)

As well as the work on the cellars themselves a living room upstairs was converted into a cloakroom and there were toilet facilities for both sexes. Mo organized the supplies and catering requirements and as the opening Saturday night drew nearer and nearer in September 1958, only two vital pieces were needed to complete the jigsaw – a name for the club and a group to open it.

It was Mo herself who had found the former, after considering several ideas. 'Why not call it the Casbah?' she said, 'you know, "come with me to the Casbah"!' She had always been taken by the old catch-phrase that derived from the 1938 Hollywood film *Algiers*, starring Charles Boyer. He had never used the actual words in the movie – 'How could I,' he commented years later, 'when I was already *in* the Casbah!' But the legend had persisted, just like the one that claimed Ingrid Bergman had said 'Play it again, Sam' in *Casablanca* when really she never did. It didn't really matter anyway. The idea was that we were going to get young people to come to *our* Casbah.

The final piece of the jigsaw proved more of a problem. Groups were sprouting up on Merseyside as rapidly as seedlings in a hothouse, but the difficulty would be in finding and being able to book the right one. A girl named Ruth Morrison, a friend of the family and one of the devoted labourers who helped get the club ready, mentioned that a friend of hers named Ken Brown might be able to help. She had got to know him at a West Derby youth club called Lowlands, where she also met one of his mates, a lad named George Harrison. Ken, she knew, played guitar and sometimes – with George – performed in a group called the Quarrymen and she had heard that they were pretty good.

John Lennon had apparently formed the Quarrymen when he was fifteen while attending Quarrybank Grammar School. Paul McCartney and George Harrison had been later recruits and Ken Brown was an occasional member, sitting in with them. In the early days the original line-up had included a tea-chest bass, but that had gone and the Quarrymen were now a trifle more sophisticated, although they had no drummer. Anyway, word was passed to Ken Brown that we were interested in the group.

Ken came along to Hayman's Green first with George in tow and told us they could make a foursome with 'a couple of friends'. The friends, of

John Lennon, aged 15, with his group the Quarrymen. Above: playing at their first date in June 1955 are (left to right) Eric Griffiths, Rod Davis, John Lennon, Pete Shotton and Len Garry. Right: playing at a local fête.

COLIN
HANTON
QUARR
MEN

course, were Lennon and McCartney. The full complement turned up at the Casbah a few days before the opening. John Lennon looked and acted the leader from the start. He had a definitely 'arty' look, dressed in a stark mixture of black and white: well-worn, bleached white pants that hugged his gangling legs like skin; a black cord lumber jacket, a black shirt; and the whole ensemble rounded off by black and white baseball boots. All the Quarrymen wore their hair swept back from their foreheads, rocker-style, but it was rather short by today's standards. The current trend was either greasy Elvis or Tony Curtis, framed by the obligatory sideboards – of course John's were longer than anyone else's. Also with the party was a pale blonde girl who was introduced to us as Cyn – Cynthia Powell, whom John had met at Liverpool College of Art and would marry some years later. That day at the Casbah they had known each other for only a short time and had recently reached the going-steady phase.

At first John was quiet, blinking around in his National Health wire-framed spectacles. But after five minutes of gazing around the pre-opening chaos of the Casbah, John made his plans, while Paul and George hovered in the background silently agreeing. A middle room, larger than most of the others except the coffee bar itself, was to be the scene of the main action and house the jukebox. 'We'll play here,' John decided, choosing a position that would put the Quarrymen in front of the jukebox – and that was the way it would be.

Those of us who were still labouring away scarcely stopped to listen in our efforts to have the Casbah ready on time, pausing only briefly, paint brushes in hand. In her usual forthright way, Mo co-opted John and told him to get to work on the ceiling, which had been white and was now in need of a coat of matt black. He set to with some initial zest, but took time out to treat us to some of his weird cartoon figures in black paint; men or women with grotesque limbs, pot-bellies and three-toed feet: always just three toes. Then they were lost for ever, obliterated by a sea of black *gloss* paint.

Because of his short-sightedness he had coated the ceiling in the wrong texture and it would cost about £50 to rectify the error. He was sorry, he said, peering contritely up through glasses that were now speckled with black paint. Never mind, we all thought, nobody's perfect.

We had already 1,000 members who had paid their money to join before the opening night – an astonishing total, considering the Casbah was nothing too ambitious or too expensive. Membership was fixed at half a crown a year (12½ pence) plus a shilling (5 pence) admission fee at the door.

As opening night approached, the excitement mounted. The doors would be unlocked at 7.30 pm that forthcoming Saturday evening and the Quarrymen would be set up and ready to make music from 8

Peter aged 16 in the garden at Hayman's Green.

o'clock. They took the engagement extremely seriously and arrived at Hayman's Green as early as 4.30 in the afternoon to make sure there would be no hitches. That evening there were fantastic scenes outside the house, with hundreds of members queueing for the big night when they would feel the first pulse of a Mersey beat destined to echo round the world.

Mo sat at a table in the foyer where the tickets were issued and the shillings changed hands; on sale were coffee, Coke, hot dogs and crisps in a room set aside as a bar, with tables and chairs, a fireplace and gleaming espresso coffee machines. Some of the paint was still a little tacky, but it did not seem to worry any of the members. There was music, laughter and happiness, which were more important. I couldn't believe this was all happening right in my home!

The Casbah quickly began to throb with the Mersey sounds that were being made nightly all around Liverpool in front parlours in pinched streets, in dingy clubs and halls – almost anywhere that could accommodate a handful of lads gathered together to make a noise that would at least please them if no one else. At this time, the Cavern Club, down in narrow little Mathew Street in the city centre, had yet to become the great Mecca of rock. It was mainly given over to traditional jazz, featuring the New Orleans styles of such British headliners as Acker Bilk, Kenny Ball and Bob Wallis with his Storeyville Jazzmen.

In our cellars the Quarrymen thrived as the weeks passed and gradually the venue would become a prime showcase for the Mersey sound. Among those who would gravitate there were Gerry and the Pacemakers, a girl named Priscilla White who found fame as Cilla Black, and Rory Storm and the Hurricanes, at that time Liverpool's best-known group, who boasted a drummer calling himself Ringo. At this stage I only knew Ringo Starr to say hello to, although later we would become friends. Rory himself – 6ft 2in in his gold lamé jacket, and known as Mr Showbusiness because of his flamboyant personality – was always the focal point and I much admired his showmanship. Cilla Black first came to the Casbah as a fan of the groups. Sometimes Rory would let her sing her 'party piece' with him – the classic Gershwin ballad *Summertime*.

It was indirectly through the Quarrymen that I became a drummer. One night, Ken Brown, who still played guitar on and off with Lennon, McCartney and Harrison, wasn't well enough to sit in with them, but when the time came to settle up, Mo included him in the Quarrymen's payout anyway. The fee was 15 shillings each (75 pence), which she handed to John, Paul and George. They became extremely annoyed and protested that the three of them should share Ken's money. 'He didn't play, so he shouldn't get paid!' they all complained. Mo would have none of it. She kept Ken's fifteen bob and gave it to him later. As Mo remembers today: 'They would fight over sixpence in those days and always insisted on being given the exact amount – and no leaving it to the next time if there was no change available.' The row led to Ken leaving the other Quarrymen, who had gone off really piqued, boycotting the Casbah for some time. It did not pose too much of a problem for there was always another group waiting in the wings.

Down in the club I'd been having a tinker at the drums from time to time. Drums had attracted me for years; I would beat out the rhythm on chairs and tables with fingers or pencils, and later drumsticks, whenever discs were on the record player at home or on the radio. At the cinema I had seen and envied the talents of jazz star Gene Krupa and had become fascinated by drums when the Casbah went into full swing. Following the 'fifteen-shilling' incident, Ken Brown came up with a suggestion that was to affect my whole life. 'Why don't we form a group of our own, Pete?' he suggested excitedly, desperate to find a way back into the business. 'Come on! You on drums.'

That was how the Blackjacks were born. It was a fun group and we had no real intention of competing with guys who were much more experienced and trying to make their living out of music. We hammered out such favourites as Chuck Berry's *Sweet Little Sixteen*, Jerry Lee Lewis's *Whole Lotta Shakin' Goin' On*, Little Richard's million-seller *Tutti Frutti* and Carl Perkins' *Honey Don't*. When we played one or two sessions at the Casbah, the customers liked us and we began to attract our own regular fans, who began to swell in number. We made so much progress that one night I was bold enough to issue a good-humoured challenge to the area's top favourite, Rory Storm with his Hurricanes.

'I bet you a pound that we can pull in more customers than you when we play the Casbah,' I said. 'You're on!' Rory grinned. The next Saturday when the Blackjacks played the Casbah was bulging – and steaming. The faithful were everywhere; cramming into the drive and into the large rear garden as well as the front, milling around shoulder to shoulder wherever there was space. It was a fantastic sight. Many of them came and went during the evening, but the overall total was an almost unbelievable 1,350. During peak-time Rory popped in and surveyed the astonishing scene for himself. He was much impressed: 'We'll have to beat that!'

On the following Saturday he was there performing with the Hurricanes and the numbers had been creeping up all during the evening. By the time the pubs had closed 1,333 bodies had checked in. 'There'll be no more now,' I told Rory during a break. 'Not this late.' He was not going to give in easily. He went out into the street to look for passers-by and offered them a shilling each to join the sweltering throng inside the Casbah. Needless to say, there were few takers in Hayman's Green at that time of the night and in the end Rory managed

The Casbah Coffee Club

(In the basement cellars of 8 Haymans Green)

Simple plan of The Casbah as it was when it first opened. As the groups became more popular, and as the Casbah membership grew, it became necessary to make a few structural alterations so that more people could get in and actually see the groups perform. This was done by removing the two walls and repositioning the entrance to the club.

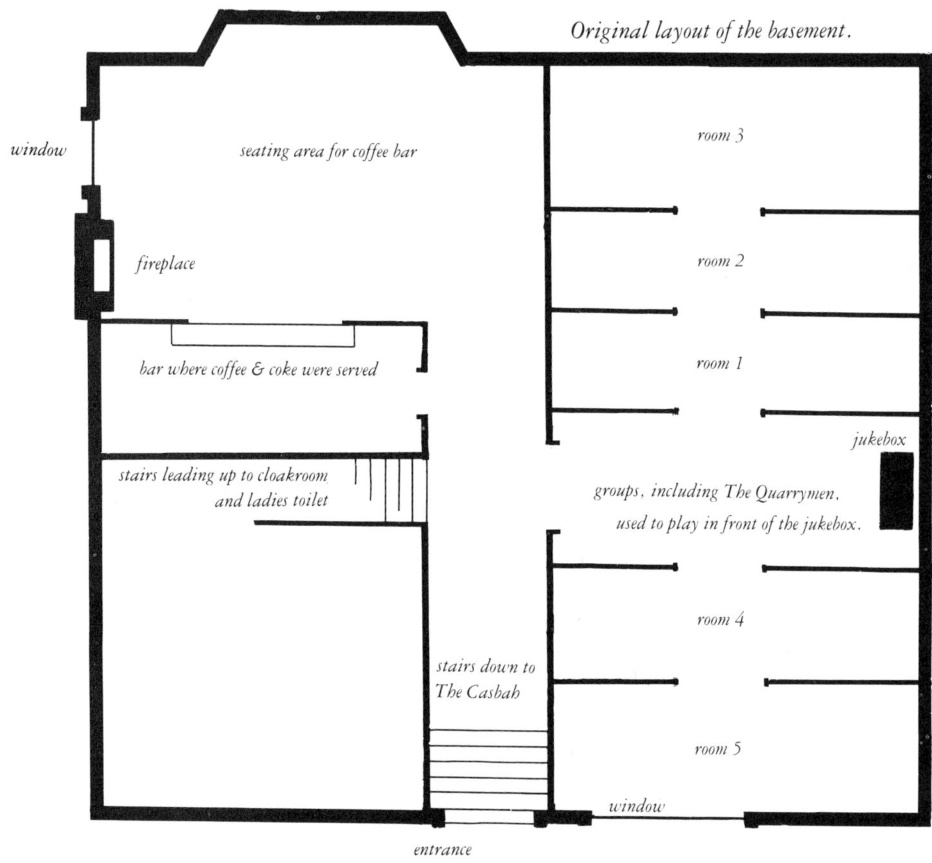

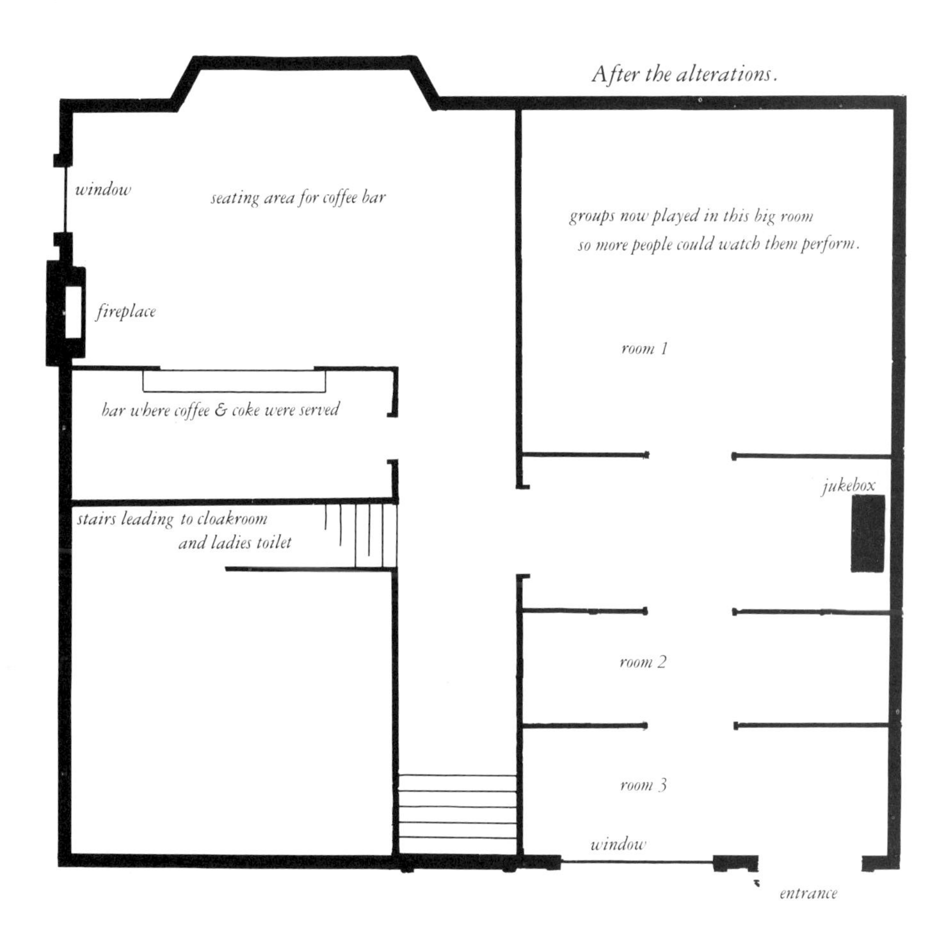

Left: Paul McCartney takes the lead at a Casbah session, backed by George Harrison, Ken Brown and John Lennon. Right: 8 Hayman's Green.

to muster a total of 1,335 paying customers – and the pound was mine.

It was all very good humoured. The Casbah was a place where innocent fun was the top priority, and people came there to enjoy themselves, the musicians as well as the young members. Among the happiest people around as the club continued to prosper were the Coca Cola salesmen. They rubbed their hands in glee every time they made a visit, for we were ordering three to four hundred crates two or three times a week. The Casbah was open all through the week, but live groups appeared only at weekends. During the week members danced to the discs they could spin in the jukebox, and all the groups took Lennon's lead, posing in front of it when they performed.

The clientele that used to home in on Hayman's Green was very mixed. The majority were teenagers who had their own favourites, either on record or in the flesh, but there was a considerable number of older members as well. You could always recognize them, even if they still looked young, because they always arrived after the pubs had closed, around 10 o'clock or even later. Very few members had cars of their own so the street was never clogged with traffic, although we did have quite a few customers arriving by motorbike.

The neighbours found very little to complain about, and some even called in to look around the club, most coming to the conclusion that it was a good meeting place for young people. Mo ensured that we were not pestered by undesirables by hiring a bouncer who would deal with any nastiness that threatened.

Life was a lot of fun as far as I was concerned. Once the club opened and its popularity grew I used to hurry home from school, race through my homework and be ready downstairs for the Casbah doors to open at 7.30 every night, whether I was playing with the Blackjacks or not.

Around the end of that year, 1958, the Quarrymen called it a day and disbanded, but they reformed the following year as Johnny (Lennon) and the Moondogs. They were only plodding along really, playing at small venues and parties and getting nowhere in the frantic race for fame. They continued to experiment with titles for the group, but it was not until 1960 that the word 'Beatle' was first mentioned. They had considered calling themselves Long John and the Silver Beatles, but rejected the first part and emerged that same year as the Silver Beatles at an audition for pop impresario Larry Parnes.

This audition was arranged for them by a Liverpool club owner and entrepreneur named Allan Williams, a stocky, curly-haired Welshman with apple-pink cheeks and a persuasive line in chat. Larry Parnes was a powerful name in British pop music in those days, boasting a rock stable which included such crowd-pullers as Tommy Steele, Marty Wilde, Billy Fury and Georgie Fame. Parnes had journeyed to Liverpool from London to look for a backing group for Billy Fury (a fellow

Liverpudlian), and for a new singer he had christened Johnny Gentle – also from Merseyside – a nineteen-year-old seaman who had serenaded passengers on luxury cruises strumming a guitar he had made himself.

At the time of the audition the Silver Beatles were using a semi-regular drummer named Tommy Moore – a man in his thirties who had drummed with them while they were the Moondogs – but he failed to show up in time for the audition and a hurried stop-gap took his place. This was Johnny Hutchinson, who was known as Johnny Hutch and played with another Liverpool group. He stepped in on this one occasion because the Silver Beatles knew that they would stand little chance without a sticks man.

Parnes has since said that the drummer did not impress him – and neither did the little fellow with dark shades and beard who appeared not to want to face the front during the all-important audition. It was understandable. He was a new recruit to the Silver Beatles named Stuart Sutcliffe, an art school friend of Lennon's who had been recruited by him. Stu, as he was known, was no great shakes as a guitarist and never pretended to be. But it so happened that he had won some money in an art competition – about enough to buy a very attractive bass guitar, with John's encouragement. Stu – a brilliant artist – had often envied his mates up there on stage and wished he could play something. Now was his chance, Lennon had said, promising that the rest of them would instruct him in easy lessons and that with experience he would soon get the hang of it.

Nevertheless, the Silver Beatles passed the audition and Parnes relented enough to include Stu in their short Scottish tour backing new-boy Johnny Gentle. Tommy Moore, now available, would be back on the drummer's perch.

It was while they were north of the border that the razor sharp Allan Williams landed a deal that would take the Silver Beatles out of Britain for the first time to their most exciting break yet – a lengthy stint in Hamburg, Germany's second largest city after Berlin.

As well as his other enterprises, Allan Williams owned a little coffee bar called the Jacaranda – a favourite haunt of Liverpool's art students, including Lennon and Sutcliffe – where a West Indian steel band had sometimes entertained customers in the basement. While his ship was in port on Merseyside an enterprising German seaman suddenly booked them into a Hamburg club, leaving Allan in the lurch. When stories of the West Indians' success in Hamburg filtered home in letters, Allan was intrigued and decided to visit Hamburg in the hope of selling other Liverpool music makers to the clubs abounding in the throbbing entertainment and vice area known as the St Pauli district.

He took with him tapes of local groups, the Silver Beatles among them (they had occasionally played at the Jacaranda) and met German club owners, among them Bruno Koschmieder – a name that would figure largely in the birth of the Beatles. Allan's tapes, however, had been badly recorded and made little or no impact on the Germans.

Back home again, Allan set about getting work for a Liverpool group called Derry and the Seniors. He travelled south to London with them to try and get them a booking at the '2 i's' coffee bar in Soho, the tiny centre of rock'n'roll which achieved international fame as the scene of Tommy Steele's discovery, and which would help spawn Cliff Richard and Adam Faith.

By an extraordinary quirk of fate, who should be hunting for talent in the '2 i's' at the same time? None other than Bruno Koschmieder, hungry for English rockers to help fill his Hamburg bars. Derry and the Seniors auditioned there and then. Bruno, impressed, booked them for his Kaiserkeller club. Their success in Hamburg led Bruno to seek more Mersey sounds, so it's not surprising that he would turn to Allan Williams to find them for him – and one of these groups was the Beatles.

Any fears that Beatle parents or guardians might have had on hearing the news of their Hamburg booking seemed to present little problem to the foursome of Lennon, McCartney, Harrison and Sutcliffe, even though they were still minors in the eyes of the law, being under the age of 21. (The legal age of majority was not reduced to eighteen until 1969.) What was far more important to them was the recurring problem of having no regular drummer. Promoters and agents wanted groups with drums; and now Tommy Moore – because of pressure from a wife or girlfriend, I was told – was giving a definite 'No' to their invitation to take off to Germany with them.

The former Quarrymen had started drifting back to the Casbah after their Scottish tour in mid-1960. George Harrison was the first to pop in, sometimes alone, sometimes with his brother Peter. The rest followed. As far as I can remember it was during June and we were about to finish school for the summer – and for ever, as it would turn out – and we all picked up where we had left off.

I was still drumming for the Blackjacks in the Casbah and was now the proud owner of a smart-looking new kit in blue mother-of-pearl which Mo had bought for me. The skins were genuine calfskin instead of the commonplace plastic and my drumming had been improving steadily. It must have made some impression on Lennon, McCartney and the others for there was a telephone call for me at the house one afternoon. 'How'd you like to come to Hamburg with the Beatles?' an excited voice asked at the other end of the line. It belonged to Paul McCartney (surprisingly, I often thought later, because John had always struck me as being the boss). It was an extremely tempting and exciting offer. The heady atmosphere at the Casbah had given me a taste for showbusiness and my original ambition to go to teachers' training college had gradually been pushed to the back of my mind.

Sitting up there behind the drums, engrossed in the rhythm, trying to sing and finding you hadn't such a bad voice after all – all this was a very pleasant experience. Even better were the applause and the girls moving in closer with big, beautiful, inviting smiles. I knew teachers' training college would never give me anything like that.

Of course, being eighteen, I too had to seek parental permission, but Mo was not going to stand in my way. The Casbah had been her idea and this musical revolution by young people for young people that was going on all round her did not have to be explained. She was part of it herself. My father, who knew all about the excitement of showbusiness, had no objections to my going off to Germany either.

The Beatles (who had by now scrapped the 'Silver' prefix) were taking no chances, however. First I had to audition at Allan Williams' Wyvern Club (later to become his popular Blue Angel Club). John Lennon was the only one there when I arrived. He played a couple of bars of *Ramrod* while I beat the skins, until George and Stu turned up and we had a further session. Paul was last, as usual, but once there they all joined in such numbers as *Shakin' All Over*. We played for about 20 minutes in all and at the end they all reached the same conclusion: 'Yeh! you're in, Pete!' Allan Williams popped in towards the finale but heard little of the actual audition.

Thus I became the fifth Beatle. Fans today still query this term whenever it appears in print, arguing that Stu was the fifth, but in strict chronological order he was the fourth.

Before setting off for the 'Fatherland' there were, naturally, the usual maternal warnings about looking after yourself and keeping your bowels regular and making sure that you always had enough to eat. But Mo is a woman of the world and she did have this to add: 'Hamburg's a wild town. Watch your step, Peter! You'll probably come back educated – a further education of a different type!' She didn't know the half of it. And sometimes I wonder if Tommy Moore, who went back to his old job of piloting a fork-lift truck at the Garston Bottle Works, would ever realize what he missed.

2

MAKING SHOW

The Jet Set would have to wait quite a time for the Beatles to join it. The trek to Hamburg was made by road and sea and took some 36 hours of discomfort, disappointment and frustration, enlivened occasionally by a few laughs, a song or two and a touch of carnival. I cannot swear to the exact date of our departure and it is not recorded in other major works on the Beatles. But I would opt for somewhere around 15–17 August, with the sixteenth as the likeliest. Some two years later 16 August would prove to be my darkest day and I would remember thinking that it was 'two years to the day'. But on this day back in 1960 there was much to look forward to.

Allan Williams decided to drive us to Germany himself in his Austin mini-bus, via the Harwich ferry to the Hook of Holland. But he didn't just take the Beatles: the passenger list totalled ten and the exercise might well have been an attempt to achieve an entry in the *Guinness Book of Records*, it was so cramped in the mini-bus. There were five Beatles, Allan, his wife and a relative, a character known as Lord Woodbine and a German chap named George Sterner, a representative of the all powerful Bruno Koschmieder. We had to stop off in London to pick him up from a Soho dive where he had been working as a waiter. Lord Woodbine was a cheerful West Indian associate of Allan's in the club business, who helped to add to the holiday mood in which we set out for what for most of us was the great unknown. And he certainly liked his Woodbines, a popular brand of cigarette at that time from which he acquired his name.

Apart from the assortment of bodies to transport there was also the formidable clutter of kit that goes with a group – instruments, amplifiers and drum kit – plus ten people's personal baggage, piled high on the roof of the minibus.

From the start our progress was anything but plain sailing. We should have had visas or permits to work in Germany so we were kept hanging around at Harwich for some five hours while Allan Williams wrangled

Pete Best at the Indra Club, Hamburg

with the port authorities. Allan – a man given to brainwaves and with a gift for sidestepping impending disaster – insisted that we were students and did not need all the interminable paper work. At last he persuaded the authorities to give way. He still says today that he 'smuggled' the Beatles into Germany as students for their first-ever appearance there.

At this stage of the great adventure we Beatles had begun to give up hope of ever getting beyond Harwich. When finally we were allowed to embark and set sail for the Hook of Holland our mood brightened considerably. Once under way we sank a few beers in the bar and strolled on deck. It was quite a long crossing, and that night we slept in the bar, stretched out on wooden benches or on the floor with coats spread over us.

Our troubles were far from over, however. The Dutch Customs people proved to be in much the same frame of mind as their Harwich counterparts. We spent at least four or more hours at the Hook of Holland going over the same familiar ground. 'But they're students!' Allan persisted. Again he got his way in the end.

Allan did most of the driving himself; once clear of Dutch Customs we headed off to Arnhem, where he wanted to see the memorial to the Allied Troops who fell during the great World War Two battle there, and the cemetery itself. The memorial, something like a long low, marble casket, bears the legend: '*Their names liveth for evermore*'. We had our pictures taken standing around it or on top of it; the words took on a prophetic new meaning that had never been intended.

After Arnhem we stopped off in Amsterdam, where John Lennon indulged in one of his light-fingered exercises. He had told me about his addiction to shop-lifting during the time I got to know him at the Casbah. 'If I ever need any stuff,' he said, 'I just go out and lift it.' When he wanted new socks or underwear he would simply make an assault on Woolworth's or Marks and Spencer and kit himself out for free.

He was wearing his favourite black cord lumber jacket – ideal wear for the nimble-fingered – as the five of us made our first exploration. We watched him as he lifted a couple of items and were amazed at how expert he was. He seemed to have a flair for it. The rest of us did not join him in trying to sneak things into our pockets, principally through fear of being caught at it, especially as this was our first trip abroad. But John was supremely confident and could easily brush aside any discouraging vision of a night being spent in a police cell. He knew what he was doing all right, and you could tell that he had done it before.

When we rejoined the rest of the party John, as blasé as ever, began to empty out his spoils. The haul amazed even those of us who had been with him on the spree. Two pieces of jewelry, a guitar string or two, handkerchiefs – and a harmonica (I can't be sure that it was the one used on *Love Me Do*, but it is possible). Allan Williams was appalled. 'You're nuts – the lot of you!' he berated us. 'The sooner we let you loose on the Germans the better!' He wanted Lennon to return the results of his afternoon's work to the rightful owners – but John wasn't made that way.

Allan himself had had an entertaining afternoon duping the Dutch people into believing that Lord Woodbine was a genuine British nobleman 'with estates in Liverpool'! As a result they were both nobly treated.

We finally set off on the last leg to Germany, the mini-bus weaving its way through the thousands of Dutch cyclists. We managed to clear the German frontier without mishap. The Beatles, fortified with beer, passed the time and miles away with a good old English sing-along that included such rousing ditties as *Rock Around The Clock* and our favourite Liverpool ballad *Maggie May*, both clean and not-so-clean versions! We had little idea of what Hamburg was like; we knew it was a large seaport like our home town and had a nightclub district where owners and managers were keen to import new British talent. But there had been no all-revealing description from Allan beforehand. Nevertheless we were on our way – and Allan managed to deliver us there without any serious mishap.

It was around nine in the evening when, as he recognized Hamburg's main railway station, the adrenalin really began to flow. 'This is it, lads!' he announced triumphantly. 'I know my way from here.'

We were due to link up with our mentor Herr Koschmieder at the Kaiserkeller, one of his clubs in the Grosse Freiheit (the words mean Great Freedom – and they can say that again), a street off the notorious Reeperbahn, main artery of the clubland area known as St Pauli.

We could only gape in sheer wonder when we hit the Reeperbahn, a jungle of neon and sex, where every other door seemed to lead to a place where girls were taking their clothes off or otherwise providing entertainment. I imagined it as being something like London's Soho, which I had never seen, but more brazen and on a much larger scale. Goggle-eyed, we watched the touts – who all wore seaman-style peaked caps – parading the wide pavements in front of garish joints that advertised girls, girls, girls! They were grabbing passers-by by the lapels or collars and almost hauling them through the entrances. There were straightforward strip palaces, dubious-looking dives, and clubs where you could sit at a table with your drink and dial-a-dame of your choice from the telephone alongside your glass.

'Here come the scousers!' we yelled at each other as we cruised past this massive array of glitter. St Pauli never really closes at any time of the day, but at nine in the evening when we were first introduced to it it was

THEIR NAME LIVETH
FOR EVERMORE

just beginning to warm up for its peak time. St Pauli became our home for weeks to come and periodically during the years ahead. It was no place to take the vicar – or Mum, come to that.

Even today in the eighties the official Hamburg tourist guide describes the Reeperbahn with total honesty. 'There are many places where one can enjoy oneself,' it says, 'but for years now there has been no strip club or show joint which can be unreservedly recommended. Without exception they are clip joints.' Describing a clip joint, the guide goes on: '... the sole object is to fleece the visitor of all his ready cash.'

However, to five fairly green young men that summer night in 1960 the St Pauli area looked like a haven of never-ending bright lights and made-to-measure pleasure. No doubt we were impressionable, being not much more than kids. At nearly twenty, Lennon was the eldest, Paul and I were both eighteen, Stu was nineteen and George still only seventeen. By law he should not have been there at all.

No one under eighteen was allowed in the St Pauli area after ten o'clock at night. We were soon to find that as the clocks everywhere ticked towards ten the police would arrive and all the lights would be turned on. They were known as the *Ausweis* patrol, *Ausweis* being the German for credentials or identity papers or cards. 'Stop the music!' the cops would order as they entered a club; then they began an inspection of all the younger-looking patrons. Every German carried an identity card giving personal details including birth date and a photograph.

No one in our party knew of this strict rule that night as we arrived, except possibly Koschmieder's man George Sterner, who obviously must have assumed that George Harrison was at least eighteen. All we could think of at that moment was a good night's kip and then getting to work as soon as possible.

Allan Williams nosed the mini-bus down the Reeperbahn to the right turn that is the cobbled Grosse Freiheit, where there were several clubs, an erotic cinema, the bizarre delights of 'ladies wrestling in mud' – and a church. It's a mystery how it came to be wedged into this blaring world of the flesh.

Our bus pulled into the kerb almost with a sigh of relief alongside the Kaiserkeller and we scrambled out and stretched our legs while we waited to collect our suitcases. Inside, the club was bright and lively and throbbing to the music of Derry and the Seniors, Allan's pioneer Liverpool group. The booze was flowing and people were enjoying themselves.

'This is a bit of all right, lads,' Lennon said, cheerfully. 'I think we're going to like it here,' agreed Paul.

After the long journey overland the warmth and excitement lifted our spirits. 'Just wait till you hear the Beatles!' was the thought uppermost in our mind, as we checked the place out, already longing to be up there

Previous page: Alan Williams' minibus is winched aboard the Harwich ferry with the Beatles' gear, en route *for Germany. Inset top: Pete at the time of the first Hamburg tour; left: at the Arnhem War Memorial, with Stu Sutcliffe (standing, in dark glasses, Allan and Beryl Williams, Lord Woodbine, (far left), and (seated, left to right) Paul McCartney, George Harrison and Pete Best; right: the Beatles, during a break between sets at the Indra.*

on stage for our first session. Then we met our patron Bruno Koschmieder; he was a heavy-set man, broad-shouldered with scarcely any neck, bushy eyebrows and an eye-catcher of a quiff that hung in rolls on his wide forehead. It was a face to be reckoned with.

Bruno wasn't much of a linguist, but the message seeped through to us pretty rapidly. 'You're not playing here,' he said, damping our enthusiasm like a fire extinguisher. 'You're going to play further along the street at the Indra.'

There was, it seemed, a right end and a wrong end of the Grosse Freiheit. The right end was immediately off the Reeperbahn itself and was a small-scale continuation of the neon world of sex, clubs and music. As you progressed along the Grosse Freiheit the lights and the attractions gradually dwindled until you found yourself at the wrong end, which was as dull as a morgue and about as inviting. This was where someone had decided to place the Indra. Our excitement began slowly to ebb away when Bruno showed us the club. It was about as lively as a cemetery chapel. The lighting was gloomy, but there was just enough of it to see that there were only two people in the place. Nothing was happening on the stage and a jukebox stood forlornly silent. It looked as if it would take a miracle to get even St Vitus to dance in here. We felt dejected and looked at each other with faces that reflected our growing misery.

'Is it open?' I asked Bruno lightheartedly, not wanting to believe that this depressing dump was to be where the Beatles were to burst on to the great German public. Hamburg had a population of more than a million and a half people, but only two of them had forced themselves to walk downstairs off the cobbles and into the Indra.

Bruno treated us to what for him was a smile. 'You boys will make the Indra into another Kaiserkeller,' he said. 'No one comes to this place,' he admitted, stating the obvious. 'But you'll make it go when you make show.'

'Make show' ... that was a phrase we were going to have to learn to live with for a long time. Bruno, in his halting English, pronounced it 'mack show', which didn't strike us as being all that amusing as we stood there like sacks of potatoes with our suitcases in hand.

'Where are we staying?' someone asked, trying to change the subject. By this time, we were all anxious to seek some escape in a comfortable night's sleep in a cosy hotel bed. Misconception number two. Bruno led the way farther along to the wrong end of the street – to a dismal cinema called the Bambi Kino which showed third-rate Westerns and the occasional sex movie. We followed him round a corner to the rear of this drab flea-pit where he opened a door which gave on to nothing but pitch darkness. We trooped through and peering through the blackness, made out a light some yards along what turned out to be a gloomy corridor. It came from a solitary light which attracted us towards it like moths; we began to run, leaving Bruno behind.

The light was coming from a room. Lennon got there first, heading the stampede, closely followed by Stu Sutcliffe, who was always somehow near John. George was just behind them and Paul and I were the last in the queue. It wasn't a pretty sight that greeted us; a scruffy, barren room containing two single beds and an ancient couch.

'What the fucking hell?' Lennon exploded.

'Fuck me!' the rest of us said, almost in unison.

John and Stu commandeered a bed each. George staked his claim on the couch. It was the old story of first come, first served. Paul and I looked at each other, wondering what the floor felt like.

Bruno had caught up with us and tried to charm us with his smile. 'But there are two more bedrooms,' he boasted; Paul and I immediately thought that possibly we were the lucky ones after all at the back of the line. A room each, we thought.

We saw them in the flickering glow of matches because these two rooms couldn't muster a solitary bulb between them. They were two dungeons, which is how we referred to them from that moment. They measured about 5ft by 6ft and most of that was taken up by a single bed on which we dumped our cases.

'You could just about swing a cat in here,' Paul observed drily – 'providing it's got no tail!' We mouthed enough obscenities to paper a wall, but Bruno either didn't understand or pretended not to. 'Only temporary,' he kept saying, 'only temporary.'

Paul sat down on his bed in the darkness and I heard the well-worn springs groan pitifully, I knew how they felt. So to bed on our first night in Hamburg, filled with disgust. The big stars from Liverpool ... The Beatles!

Even in the daytime, we found, there was no light. Our billet was an extension built on to the rear of the cinema – right next to the toilets! We had to wash and shave in cold water in the cinema urinals – where sometimes the patrons of the Bambi Kino would surprise us and stand and stare at the haggard, black and white apparitions. Lennon, George and Stu were living in comparative luxury in their drab three-bed room some 25 yards along a corridor. Bruno's 'only temporary' promise never did come true. We were doomed to the dungeons, which became home, stacked with guitar and drum cases and a collection of old laundry.

Paul and I never knew if it was night or day. We wrote letters home sitting on our beds with pocket torches strapped round our heads like miners' lamps. Day after day we all complained to Bruno about the dingy squalor in which we were living. We pointed out that we were, after all, lads from decent middle-class backgrounds whose parents had scrimped and worked to try to give us a good education. What had we done to end up in Germany being treated like a bunch of dossers or winos ready to kip down anywhere for a night? Daily we were given the same smarmy smile and promises, promises. Bruno had once been a clown, we were told, but he certainly didn't make us laugh.

On the opening night at the Indra a reasonable crowd turned up to cast a critical eye on the new boy wonders from Liverpool. Acoustically, it was like playing under a pile of bedclothes. There were drapes everywhere – probably because the Indra had once been a strip club – and they killed the sound in its tracks. We took to the stage in the depths of depression. Bruno, very much in evidence, yelled at us that we must 'make show', which we did, more as a release for our mounting anger rather than to please him.

'All the way from Liverpool to leap around like a lot of idiots!' Lennon summed up. For that's what 'making show' was all about – jumping around aimlessly, stamping, writhing on the floor. None of us had ever acted the fool like this on stage before.

Hitherto, groups had generally stood and played somewhat in the style of Cliff Richard's Shadows, with their neat little coordinated footsteps and gentle swaying, which was never allowed to get in the way of the music. Of course there had been the cavortings of Bill Haley and his Comets, jumping around or lying on their backs still playing their instruments, which had all seemed a bit daft, and the piano gymnastics of Jerry Lee Lewis, who exploded like a firework in his act. But it wasn't for us.

Anyway, our repertoire was not exclusively rock'n'roll and we were playing several middle-of-the-road offerings. Paul was into *Somewhere Over The Rainbow* and other syrupy numbers. We used to do *Red Sails In The Sunset* and *Ain't She Sweet*. No wonder when the time came a lot of major record companies slammed the door in our faces. But this was the start and we had a lot to learn. 'Make show', Bruno had ordered with his usual Germanic charm. So we did. Like five bloody lunatics.

We went from one extreme to the other. John and Paul were the looniest. John did his best to imitate Gene Vincent, grabbing up the microphone as if he were going to lay into the audience with it, carrying it around with him, leaping about with it like a maniac. Paul roared around screaming like Little Richard and, as the days passed, an act developed.

Stu behaved something like a puppet and managed to hold on to the sort of James Dean image he had fostered, quietly trying to stay cool in the background behind his dark shades. There was not much I could do from behind the drums other than stand up and hop around the kit with a tom-tom under my arm. George paid serious attention to his guitar-playing, trying to prevent the sets from becoming too ridiculous.

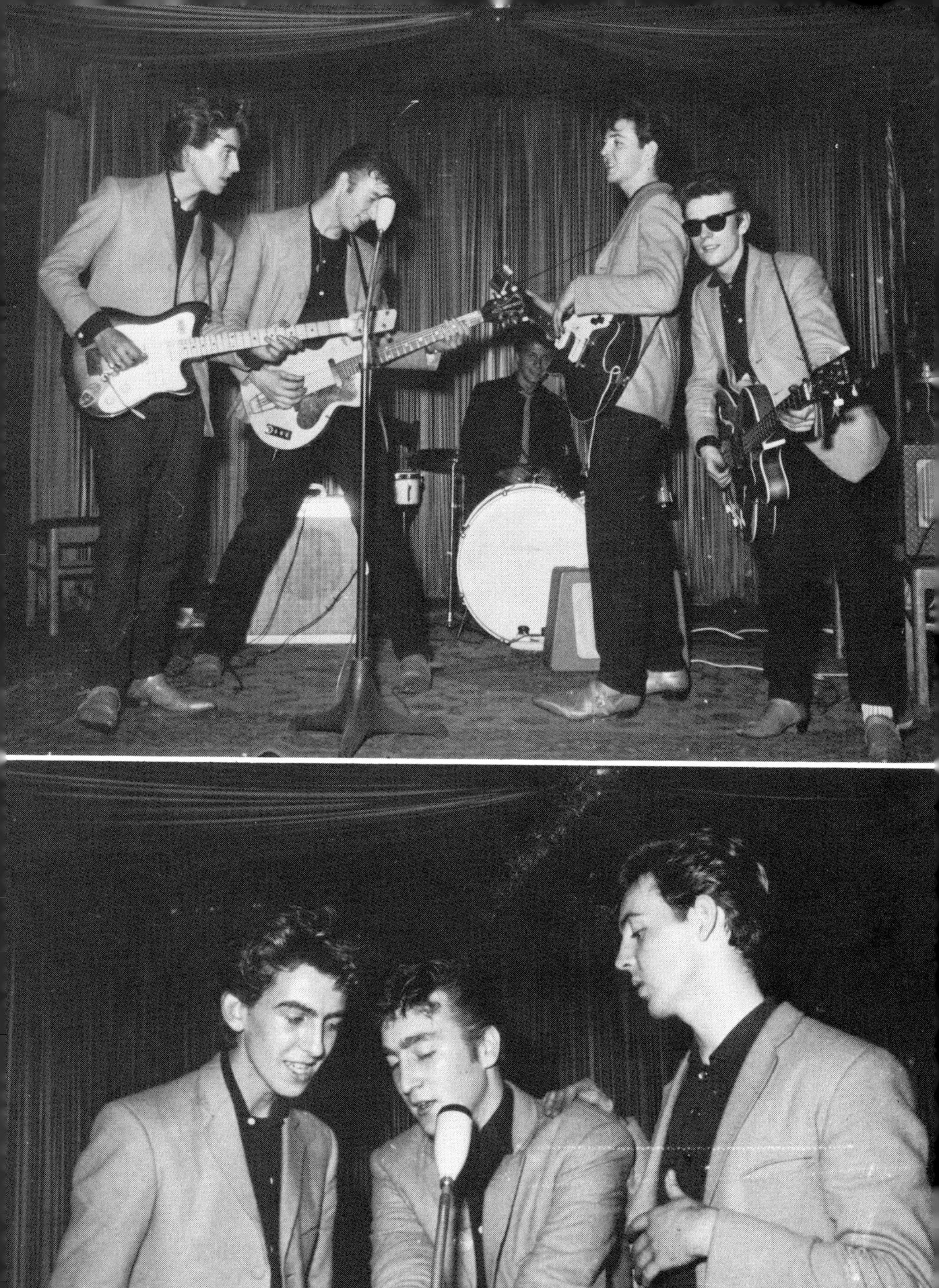

The German rockers loved it and no one realized – least of all Bruno – that we were trying to take the piss out of them. But in the end it worked against us. This was the Beatles developing, creating excitement. 'Making show' would eventually take us over. However, at first it was a protest for the treatment we were receiving, letting ourselves rip because of the lousy digs and the sub-survival wages of £15 a week each.

We had one number we used to put in that began very slowly and sounded like smooch music. The audience would take to the floor and get all cuddly and close, then suddenly we would erupt into a frenzied rock tempo. At first it took the Germans by surprise – to us it was another form of protest – but then they started to request the song where we changed gear in mid-stream! Another back fire.

We used to stomp around half crazed for more than seven hours a night. Making show? You've never seen anything like it. Sometimes Paul wouldn't even have his guitar plugged in, but no one noticed the omission with all the noise that went on. John used to roll around on stage when he wasn't throwing the mike in the air; then he would twist himself into a hunch-back pose. By way of a change he would jump on to Paul's back and charge at George and Stu and send them reeling. Sometimes they would give each other piggy-backs. What little music there was would be made by George and Stu and most of that was simply rhythm. Other times John would hurl himself into a sort of flying ballet leap from the stage into the audience and end up doing the splits.

While the audience was dancing, John and Paul often jumped down from the stage and bundled into them like wild bulls; or maybe they would do a ring-of-roses with them. But this is what the punters wanted and had paid money for. They didn't want to sit around and listen to original Beatles' music – not that a lot of it existed at this stage – and it was obvious that they appreciated the outrageous slapstick rather than the musicianship. They started to call us the *beknakked* Beatles – a German slang word that described us as the mad or crazy Beatles – but we never stopped to worry about it.

The songs were exclusively American; Fats Domino and Carl Perkins numbers, along with Gene Vincent, Elvis and Little Richard hits. The Germans loved the Ray Charles classic *What'd I say*, which really lent itself to audience participation. They would echo the lyrics and keep time to the beat, banging their bottles on the tables.

Many of the stories that have been told over the years about the way we used to behave on stage allege that the Beatles used to have serious fights in front of the audiences. This wasn't strictly true: a lot of it was just part of 'making show'. What used to appear to be a brawl on stage began at the Indra, where nightly we began to take more liberties in the cause of 'making show'. Paul, with possibly only one string on an

The Beatles on stage at the Indra. Top left: Learning to 'make show'. Below left: adjusting the mike.

unplugged guitar, would rush up to John while he was singing and pretend to butt him. Feigning anger, Lennon would retaliate. It must have all appeared to be very real to the patrons and used to wind them up, but it was sheer pretence, a mock battle in which nobody was hurt. In those early days we were extremely close and the best of friends at all times and we would go through much together in the spirit of five rather seedy musketeers.

There is no doubt that John and Paul gave their all to 'making show' – even if they did find it a release from the frustrations besetting us all. Lennon gradually became bolder with each week that passed, haranguing the paying customers as 'fucking Krauts', or Nazis or Hitlerites. Later he extended this repertoire of venom to 'German spassies' (spastics), indulging in his obsession with the disabled which would later manifest itself more publicly in his writings, drawings and statements during interviews. For their part, the Germans, whom he also advised to 'get up and dance, you lazy bastards!', rarely showed any signs of understanding and would often applaud his insults.

Indulging his cripple fantasies on stage, he would twist himself into grotesque shapes which were far more comprehensible and which not everyone in the audience appreciated. But what other people thought of Lennon rarely caused him concern. Yet the mere sight of deformed or disabled people sickened him physically and he could never bear to be in their company. More than once I was with him in a Hamburg cafe when suddenly he would discover that the occupant of a nearby table was a war veteran, minus a limb or disfigured in some way. John would leap up from his seat and scurry out into the street. On one occasion I saw this happen even after he had already ordered a meal and was about to be served.

He never tried to explain this odd behaviour or his reasons for devoting so much of his artistic talent to depicting distorted characters. Somewhere deep down I felt that perhaps he nursed a sort of sadness for them.

More and more people were now seeking their entertainment at the Indra as the news of the mad, bad Beatles buzzed through the city. Within a month we had become a hit group with our interpretation of 'making show', with its sham fights, crazy horse-play and John's earthy advice.

He gave many people in the audiences the impression that he was a buffoon, but what he did on stage was simply a form of escapism for him. He played the idiot who shouted his mouth off and yelled obscenities but was the outright victor in any slanging match. It was the kind of behaviour they came to expect of him. After these bitter attacks on the people who were paying our wages Lennon would simmer down as though he had just aired some long pent-up grievance and was relieved to have got it off his chest.

I used to try and explain this abuse of audiences to myself but could only conclude that John harboured no deep hatred of the Germans and that they were simply the scapegoats for his increasing frustration at having to entertain them in a fashion that really wasn't his style.

At the Indra we acquired a friend who would stand by the Beatles for a long time to come. She was the lavatory attendant, a lady whom we christened Mutti. Anyone over the age of twenty seemed old to us, but I reckon Mutti must have been in her fifties, hence our nickname for her, sounding something like the German word for mother – *Mutter*. She was in nightly attendance backstage, where our poky dressing room adjoined the toilets (where else?). When we came off stage she would be waiting for the perspiring Beatles with towels and paper napkins and changes of shirt, which was very necessary after the rigours of 'making show'.

Almost nightly as well she had to prepare a needle and thread for John to repair his pants after his dare-devil Nureyev leaps. But he always insisted on making his own renovations, just sitting there in his underpants, sewing away and using something like sailor's tacks and a few reef knots. (Needless to say the repair would give way after the next performance!) If anyone arrived backstage – male or female – while he was working away in his underwear he would simply invite them to 'come in and make yourself at home' and continue with the task.

By this time we were drinking more than our fair share of Hamburg's booze. It came by the crate and we drank on stage, as well as clowned. The Germans were extremely generous and recognized that 'making show' could create an enormous thirst. Some of the dedicated regulars were ever deserting the Kaiserkeller now to catch the Beatles at the Indra. Not that Bruno minded. We were giving him what he wanted and achieving his objective for the Indra – to make it as popular as his other club.

If there had been any rivalry, it all ceased two months after we first opened at the Indra, when Bruno gave us the news: 'The Indra's got to close!' 'Why?' we inquired anxiously. 'Because of the noise!' we were informed. We were all disappointed and confused. We had worked like maniacs to build the club up from nothing – and now it was going to shut down due to the din of 'making show'! It was ironic. Apparently Koschmieder had been warned several times by the police that the Indra would have to close if the noise continued. He ignored them and we carried on blissfully unaware of the threat. He knew, however, that the police would eventually lose patience, and he had warned us only just in time.

The end came very suddenly after Bruno's announcement. We arrived one night as usual to find that the Indra had been closed by the

TRUVOICE

A publicity shot for the Indra – with the Beatles showing their feelings! Left to right: John, George, Pete, Paul and Stu.

cops. Bruno was obviously more annoyed than we were, but there was nothing he could do about it. Residents living opposite or nearby the club at this wrong end of the Grosse Freiheit had been complaining bitterly and the madness had to cease – by order. Yet strangely an old lady who lived directly above the club in an apartment never did moan to the police. She was either deaf or a latter-day rocker.

Even if this was the end of the Indra it was by no means the end of the Beatles in Hamburg. Bruno, who was now openly pleased at the results of our endeavours, wasn't prepared to let us go that easily (our initial contract with him was for two months and could be extended verbally). He decided to move us along the street to the Kaiserkeller and thus help pack more people in. Here John would be able to improve on his ballet act. The Kaiserkeller boasted a piano on stage and he would climb on top of it, stomp around, then fling himself with a sensational leap into the customers.

Somehow the Kaiserkeller seemed to bring out the best and worst in Lennon. One night he appeared on stage in his underpants in a knockabout impression of Hitler, a toilet seat round his neck, a broom for martial effect and chanting '*Sieg heil! Sieg heil!*' If anyone objected to what he was doing they would be told to get stuffed. Sometimes the rest of us used to enter into the spirit by daring him to be even more outrageous.

As winter approached at the Kaiserkeller he bought himself a baggy pair of long johns in an effort to keep warm. Late one Saturday night when he was sitting in them in his lousy room behind the Bambi Kino, writing a letter to Cynthia, George said: 'I dare you to go out and stand in the Grosse Freheit in those!'

Lennon didn't hesitate. He picked up an English newspaper he had been reading earlier, tucked it under one arm, kicked open the crash doors, strode out into the middle of the street – crowded with weekend visitors to St Pauli – and just stood there reading the paper.

Then, after several minutes, he folded it, put it under his arm again, came to attention with a Nazi click of the heels, gave the Hitler salute, said goodnight in German to the onlookers and marched back inside with a deadpan face. Paul, George and I watched the whole episode, peering round the edge of the doorway, but John never received any reward from us when he carried through one of our dares.

I can't remember which one of us challenged him to bare his bottom on stage. The bandroom at the Kaiserkeller was near the entrance and to get to the stage we had to walk through the audience. This night John changed into a pair of navy-blue swimming trunks and marched straight-faced to the stand with his guitar. In the middle of *Long Tall Sally* he turned round and, with his back to the audience, dropped his trunks to reveal all.

His rear was only a foot away from the customers, so close that they could have kissed his ass. But no one did. There was some laughter but no comment at all from the Kaiserkeller patrons.

When we opened there we doubled on the bill with Derry and the Seniors. Later we were reunited with our old pal Rory Storm, who still had this fellow Ringo Starr drumming for him with the Hurricanes. It was on this first trip to Hamburg that he and I really got to know each other. Drummers tend to pal up and talk about their trade and equipment. This happened in a minor way in England before we went to Germany, when we both attended a memorial show for Eddie Cochran at Liverpool Stadium. But it was in Germany that the friendship blossomed.

We reached the stage where we would lend one another drumsticks and go shopping together for items of kit such as cymbals. It was an extremely pleasant relationship that would last for a long time to come, but not for always.

ABARIN
HOLSTEN-BIER
MOU

3

LOVE'S FREE FOR ALL

The St Pauli area of Hamburg in the early sixties must have been something like Chicago in the twenties; it was a crazy, non-stop world of birds, booze and the big beat and Gangsterism was rife as well. Most of the clubs were controlled by racketeers, and top mobsters watched over the vast trade in prostitution and drug peddling. Pimping was big business, along with perversion and pornography. There were mob battles, beatings-up and sometimes murders, although nothing quite on the scale of Chicago's infamous St Valentine's Day massacre of 1929.

We were strongly advised to be extremely careful at all times. 'Watch your step. Once you make an enemy – that's it!' we were warned more than once by friendly Germans. It was good advice. We soon learned it was important to get in with the call girls and other prostitutes but the most important people in Hamburg to have on your side were the waiters.

It seemed that these men came from a special breed: mostly squat, broad of shoulder and as rough and tough as any character in a gangland movie. Experts at waiting at table, they doubled as strong-arm men and bouncers with equal dexterity.

Stock issue for all waiters was a spring-loaded truncheon. It was weighted and kept handy in the most accessible pocket. When trouble loomed they would immediately reach for their truncheons which leapt into life on their springs and were ready to smash in a head or two. It was an essential weapon for dealing with the nightly clubland brawls. But waiters did not only use truncheons; neatly tucked into the back of trousers, and hidden by their jackets, they kept tear gas guns that would be used when fights got out of hand and threatened to develop into a riot.

At close range a gas gun could inflict a lot of pain; it could damage your eyes, making them water uncontrollably, while they smarted until you felt like tearing them out. The gas could also cause burns and scorching and attacked the nerves in your nostrils. The guns came in

Night-life in Hamburg's St Pauli district.

varying sizes, but the most popular type was black and looked very much like a bullet firing pistol. Some models were single-loading, others secreted a clip of cartridges in the butt in the fashion of the Luger pistol. You would never suspect that they fired anything but lethal slugs of lead until someone squeezed the trigger.

The ladies of St Pauli – strippers, call girls, prostitutes – carried smaller, chic pearl-handled types in their handbags. Indeed many St Pauli residents never went out without a gas gun, even some of the cash customers for sex who feared that they might be stripped of more than their pants. None of the Beatles ever owned one during the two years that Hamburg was our periodic second home. We fired them all right – but just for fun. The first time was after we had moved to the Kaiserkeller, where the waiters let us try out theirs. We harmlessly pumped off a few rounds outside a rear door, then quickly closed it before the gas cloud could start taking any effect. Unlike guns that fire bullets, in a breeze these could get their own back on you.

You can see why a waiter could be a lad's best friend, especially if you were a green newcomer from England. Luckily for us the Beatles made many useful friends among the waiting fraternity. It was a waiter who first put us wise about some of the girls who started to make a play for us during the early days at the Indra Club. We found ourselves pulling birds without any effort and indulging in almost limitless sex with them in our humble dungeons. There were even quickie sessions in the cramped backstage area during our fifteen minute break between sets.

As far as we knew, they were ardent fans or groupies demonstrating their devotion to the barmy Beatles whom they had taken to their hearts. Some of them were. But we soon learned that others were high-class call girls and prostitutes having their own fun and games on their nights out – without as much as a pfennig changing hands.

A smiling waiter made the revelation one night at the Indra. 'You know,' he said, like an agent passing on a secret, 'you can see some of these girls in their shop windows!'

'Shop windows?' 'What are they then – fashion models?' 'Where?' we clamoured, our imaginations working overtime.

'In the Herbertstrasse!' he said with a knowing air.

The name didn't mean anything to us. It was a street only five minutes' walk from the Grosse Freiheit, off the Reeperbahn, but so far we hadn't had time to explore much, pounding out music seven and sometimes eight hours a night, every night of the week including Sunday. But this we had to see. We set forth in a posse early one morning – well, early for us, around eleven o'clock – to discover the Herbertstrasse, still intrigued by the waiter's parting words: 'You can window-shop there all day long and you don't have to pay a thing so long as you only window-shop!'

The Herbertstrasse is one of the strangest streets in the world, sealed off at either end by tall barriers erected like screens. You cannot see anything inside the street until you slip through the entrance, which was similar to those of some old public urinals in Britain.

There was an official notice prominently displayed at the entrance which said that no one under the age of eighteen was allowed into this street of secrets, which meant that George immediately came under a barrage of ribbing from the rest of us.

'No, George!' Lennon mocked, holding him back with a restraining arm, 'you can't come in with us *men*!' 'You're still only a baby!' we chided him. Relenting in the end, we promised to 'smuggle' him in, and we all trooped through the entrance.

It was an extraordinary sight. There wasn't a shop in view, just a street made up of cosy little flatlets – that's how they struck me – each with a girl in the window. The only shopping you could do in the Herbertstrasse was for sex. The girls perched in their windows at sill-level to give one an overall view, displaying themselves on tables or on chairs, demonstrating the wares available in an assortment of seductive poses. And what goods!

These were not just any old scrubbers or slags. There were blondes, brunettes and redheads in various stages of dress or undress; some of them voluptuous and slinky; many with luscious legs and breasts. They were like pin-up tableaux or pages from girlie magazines come to life. We stood before them enraptured. And sure enough there would be some that we recognized and who would recognize us in turn with wide beaming smiles. But what first caught our interest near the entrance was a giant of a woman in one window, the owner of probably the biggest boobs in the world, which seemed to be trying to fight their way out of a set of black stays. Her sturdy legs were encased in black leather thigh boots – and in one hand she gripped a whip! She was unbelievable.

After staring at her open-mouthed, we moved on to discover one of our friends from the Indra. She squealed with delight: 'Come on in – for free!' But we didn't take up the offer. Though it was before midday, there were already quite a few paying customers around, males of all ages surveying the flesh like gourmets shopping for a prime cut of beef.

Some of them began to follow us and we in return became a little more adventurous, actually treating them and the girls to a display of 'making show', clowning about, jumping, leaping, lying down on the cobbles and making goo-goo eyes at the tantalizing offerings in the windows.

Surprisingly, we learned, this bizarre street was strictly controlled by the Hamburg police, who saw that the girls had a clean bill of health among other things, and protected them from unscrupulous pimps.

Even today, more than twenty years later, the official tourist guide states that 'if you're looking for a girl ... your safest bet is still the Herbertstrasse'.

After our first sortie down the Herbertstrasse, window-shopping there became a daily routine for us. We used the street as a short cut to another of the city's delights – the British Seaman's Mission down on the quayside, where we could tuck into meals more like the ones we were used to at home and eat our way through packets of cornflakes. We were cornflake buffs. But it wasn't really a short cut through the Herbertstrasse; that was just our excuse. In fact it was rather a long way round to go to the quay; our daily visit was really a courtesy call on the ladies in the windows. We described this regular excursion as 'our morning booster'.

We introduced Rory Storm to the street, managing to spring it on to him as a complete surprise. We simply invited him to come with us one morning 'to have some cornflakes at the seamen's mission'. He was marched smartly through the entrance to the Herbertstrasse without any prior warning of what was to be found inside.

Rory was overwhelmed and took about twenty lingering minutes to get beyond the first window. 'Come on!' we goaded him, 'the cornflakes will be getting cold.'

God knows what the folks back home in Liverpool would have thought if they could have seen us then. Most of us had received some kind of pep talk like mine before we left, however brief. But not one parent or John's guardian Aunt Mimi could ever have imagined the life we would lead. Our parents were probably reconciled to the adventure in the first place because it seemed that Allan Williams would be coming along as our chaperone. But he stayed on with us for only a short time before returning to Merseyside and I doubt if even he realized that he would lead us into a situation that would develop into the realms of the Arabian Nights.

After we had become daily sightseers in the Herbertstrasse, more of the girls from the windows came to see us perform at the Indra and later the Kaiserkeller. And they always made it plain that their much sought-after services would be available to the Beatles without any fee. I still remember some of their names: Greta, Griselde, Hilde, Betsy, Ruth... They were nice ladies, all of them. We became accustomed to seeing them in the windows with nothing or next to nothing on, but when they ventured into the night club on an evening off duty they were immaculately dressed like Paris models, way ahead of the dolly birds – the Beatles' first groupies – who were also willing to jump into bed with us at any time.

The Herbertstrasse girls used to take a seat in the club and order drinks for the boys in the band. The waiters would deliver them to us on stage with the message that 'this is from Greta', or whoever it might be, and we would have to toast the girl – even in the middle of a number – or she would show extreme annoyance. As we raised our glasses, she would put up a dainty, elegant hand and wave in acknowledgement. They would also become irritated if we didn't find time to talk to them. If this happened they would close their curtains or shutters when we approached their windows in the Herbertstrasse next day.

During our daily jaunts through the street the outsize lady with the big boobs and whip became our favourite. She would always rise from her seat whenever she saw the Beatles coming. We stood like kids gazing at lollipops – pulling the ugliest faces in the world at her. Then she would lash out with her whip and pretend to try to beat us with it and we would all take our jackets off. But it was all in good humour and our Herbertstrasse clowning probably drummed up quite a bit of business for some of the occupants in the windows.

Taunting George about being under age also became a daily routine. Sometimes we would make him stay outside for five minutes or so, one of us keeping guard – as a sort of mock penalty for still being a kid.

Frequently we would be guests at the girls' parties, usually held in their own apartments away from the Herbertstrasse. Or they would invite us to shindigs being given by someone else, possibly a big-spending patron. They were lavish occasions and the drink flowed as if Prohibition was going to start tomorrow. It was just as well that much of our booze and love came free. As soon as we received our meagre pay packets from Bruno Koschmieder we would immediately blow it. Next to sex, drink was our main pastime. We weren't into museums.

In those early days, when we first became aware that there were girls who would do anything for us, we used to wonder where we could take them for a session of love-making if they were unable to provide a venue of their own. How could we possibly invite a dame to our squalid digs alongside the cinema urinals, dark and damp as a sewer and about as attractive? But we did, and not one girl ever said no. In time, at our quarters behind the Bambi Kino, the orgy became a nightly ritual for Lennon, McCartney, Harrison and Best – for Stu Sutcliffe was no longer in residence. Within a few weeks of our arrival in Hamburg he had met and fallen in love with a German beauty named Astrid – another person who would have much influence on the emergence of the Beatles. Stu was given a room of his own in her parents' home and George moved off the miserable couch and inherited his bed near John. In the space of two months Stu would become engaged.

Meanwhile Paul and I sometimes experienced a little difficulty in persuading the birds through the darkness into our five-by-six cells. But somehow love would always find a way. John and George were more fortunate in their larger room with its one light. However, we shared everything in those days, and for the nightly romp there were usually five or six girls between the four of us. During the proceedings there would come an echoing cry from John or George along the corridor enquiring of Paul and me: 'How's yours going? I'm just finishing. How about swapping over?' 'How you two doing? I fancy one of yours now!' The girls would each do the rounds with us. It was a case of change partners, but no dancing.

Birds, ready, willing and able, were vying for our attention everywhere – not only at the club at which we were appearing. They would even trail us to our eating haunts. We often called in for a bite at a cafe called Harold's, and admiring girls would be there, happy to buy us meals – and give other delights for free later. We certainly needed sustenance; we found ourselves having two or three girls a night each, depending on how fit we were. The most memorable night of love in our dowdy billet was when eight birds gathered there to do the Beatles a favour. They managed to swap with all four of us – twice! It has to be a record. It certainly was for us during our Hamburg tours.

There were nights when we felt so bushed that all we wanted to do was head back to the dungeons and hit the sack. Even these sordid surroundings could be something to look forward to when you felt nearly on your knees. But we couldn't win. I would reach my cupboard-like room ready to flop – and find that there was a bird already waiting outside my door. Some of them had discovered that they could enter our quarters through the cinema: all they had to do was buy a ticket, then head for the toilets, push open a crashbar on a door and there they would be at the Beatles' undersirable residence.

When Paul and I would arrive at our doors we would hear sniggering in the darkness and suddenly become aware of the aroma of perfume – and it was a case of doing justice, no matter how we felt. Sometimes we never even saw the face of the girl who had waited in the gloom to share our beds. Perhaps I would light a match or flick on a torch if I had remembered to carry one with me – and discover my cookie was about five-feet six, blonde and had enough of what it took to keep a tired Beatle awake. (I don't recall any ugly ones.)

If the whole business took place in complete darkness – and sometimes it did – there was one way of finding who the girl was next day. There she would be in the audience at the club with a big satisfied smile on her face, chatting with a bunch of her fraulein friends, and casting a sly look your way.

Down at the club, if a young fraulein fancied one of us she would sit by the stage at a point nearest the Beatle she had in mind for the night's festivities. If you didn't somehow signal your approval by a wink or a nod, the girl might make her intentions more obvious by sliding a hand out to touch you. While we were in the middle of some solid rock number one of us would feel a finger on our leg. There was no thinking twice about what it meant.

Some nights the gathering of girls near the stage planning to rendezvous with me would be quite considerable. 'You're a bit lop-sided tonight, Pete!' one of the other Beatles would gag. The more brazen of the girls didn't even bother to get near to you on stage or try to touch you. She would simply stand up and point at the Beatle she wanted and give the well-known sign. You know it – the bending of the elbow of one arm across the wrist of the other in a sharp upward movement that suggests an erection.

'Wheeee!' the girl would shout at the same time. Or later, as they got to know us more intimately, 'Gazunka!', which was the Beatles' own war cry. We would fall about on stage whenever a fraulein gave out this routine, but she was never kidding.

There were nights when all four of us would be royally entertained by girls in surroundings far more luxurious than usual. There was one flat to which we would be taken that had more than a dozen rooms – most of them bedrooms. Once we had passed through the front door we would receive our orders. 'You're in Bedroom One,' you would be told. 'You're in Number Four!' Again there was never anything to pay for.

The top-class call girls were more discreet in their approach, sending their invitations via a waiter, accompanied by a beer and a glass of schnapps as a gesture of goodwill. These ladies would sometimes take us for a meal beforehand, then we would go to their places. Most of them were known to the waiters – whose knowledge of the frauleins of the Reeperbahn and St Pauli was so thorough that they were even able to brief us on the sexual foibles of our hostesses, right down to their favouorite positions for the sex act. 'This one likes it with her boots on,' was the kind of advice we would receive from a waiter. Or maybe she was 'hung up about leather...'

Professional girls and others used to swamp us with presents – as well as feed us and pay for our booze. In the morning at the Seaman's Mission while we were nose-bagging into the cornflakes, we would exchange stories of the night's exploits. 'How was yours?' was the frequent opening line. When one Beatle would confess that he had run out of steam during the proceedings he would be advised to prepare himself with more cornflakes!

John was the one who set the breakneck pace at which we lived. Maybe he felt less inhibited than the rest of us; he had no parental ties and was well away from the scoldings he used to say that Aunt Mimi gave him. He could do exactly as he liked and be as outrageous as he wished. In those hectic days we all had a healthy appetite for sex, but

Lennon's was stronger than most. Sexually, Hamburg was a young man's dream – we were surrounded by it and it was available round the clock. Even so John would proudly find energy enough to masturbate as well, never trying to keep it a secret. He would lock himself away for five minutes with some soft-porn pin up studies and then rejoin the rest of the Beatles with a satisfied grin on his face.

'That was very good!' he would report in all honesty, frequently pointing out that he was a 'randy sod'.

During one of our sets, if he suddenly found himself attracted by a girl in the audience he would go through masturbatory motions with one hand in full view of everyone, not giving a cuss.

John didn't like his sex to be too conventional and would regale us with details of his experiments with such comments as 'I had her over a chair'. Sometimes it would be a table; or, 'I tried position 68, with her standing on her head in the corner!' There was no reason to disbelieve him, he was always honest about his sexual activities. 'The more the merrier' he would laugh if he had been able to go to bed with two or three girls at one time.

Fortunately we all learned one vital lesson at the Roxy Bar on the Reeperbahn, where you could easily be fooled into thinking that you were getting the come-on from some of the most gorgeous girls in all Germany. In fact every one of them was a transvestite on some kind of game – a fact that we were unaware of the first time we were introduced there by a German friend. He warned us just in time of the consequences of getting acquainted. It was very much to the point.

'If you don't go to bed with them' he said, 'they'll kick shit out of you!' We never gave them the opportunity.

4

MONEY AND MAYHEM

Every night was a hard day's night during the first Beatle invasion of Hamburg. Life was generally becoming a struggle as winter arrived, bringing with it the bitter weather that sweeps down from the Russian Arctic. We felt the draught in more ways than one. Herr Koschmieder was by now certainly proving he was not a man of his word. He had promised us more reasonable accommodation several times, but we were still in the same old flea-bags behind the Bambi Kino in conditions that were now tugging at our nerves. He had promised us more cash if and when we transformed the Indra into a magnet similar to the Kaiserkeller. But no raise was forthcoming, not even when we were responsible for increasing the take at this second rendezvous. He was adamant about it. When he said no, he meant no. Trying to get money out of Bruno Koschmieder was like trying to extract a blood sample from a rocking horse.

Bruno even accused us of deliberately breaking up the stage at the Kaiserkeller with all the 'making show' he had demanded in the first place. It was a lousy old stage, little more than planks on beer crates or orange boxes. True, we went through it with all the leaping around and eventually ended up playing on the floor. Yet Bruno was serious. He actually stopped £5 each from our pay packets for destroying the stage!

When November came and the cold really began to bite, the Beatles – with the exception of Stu – were at a low ebb. Stu and Astrid were now very much in love and in this month exchanged rings to mark their engagement. He was leading a vastly different life to the rest of us, well away from the garish vulgarities of St Pauli. As a result he came in for a good deal of barracking from the rest of us. He had been on the receiving end even before meeting Astrid, being the smallest of the five Beatles, which made him something of an easy target. Then, falling in love with a nice middle-class girl when the rest of us seemed to be sharing our virility with half the female population of the great seaport city only served to make him more of a sitting duck.

Much of the banter was good-natured although, in retrospect, it must have been extremely aggravating at times. Stu had chosen to follow a more satisfying path while we were rolling round Hamburg boozing and birding and kidding ourselves that life was good when, in fact, it was simply a charade that was now wearing thin. There were days when we went hungry, missing out on meals, even though admirers were still buying us the occasional feed. And we were in need of clothing as well as sustenance. Our plight was such that we felt little shame in asking girl fans to help save on the laundry bills by washing our jeans and shirts and underwear. They willingly took to the task.

We had all the sex in the world. Money, however, was the commodity we were short of most. We talked about it frequently and tried to plan ways to raise more, but we needed it quickly and any long-term scheme would be useless. Yet there had to be some way other than holding up a bank.

The chance came one night when into the Kaiserkeller there stepped a real big spender, a German sailor who had to be the possessor of one of the fattest wallets in town. He was a husky guy in his mid to late thirties, we guessed, with shoulders like an ox. And he enjoyed our music so much that he sent us all a drink on stage. Then another one – and another one! This was the kind of fan to have when you were broke. As the night wore on he dispatched a waiter to the stage with a message for us as well as the usual beer and schnapps. 'He's so happy with the Beatles,' the waiter said, 'that he wants to take you out to have a meal after the session is over.'

Four of us took up the invitation: Stu would go home with Astrid as he always did. The rest of us relished the thought of a big nosh-up for free. At the restaurant the sailor kept the booze flowing freely and the atmosphere was very friendly, and that wallet was certainly fat when he produced it at the table. We all peered at it intently, fascinated. This was temptation, staring us squarely in the face. Drunken sailors had always been considered fair game in Hamburg amongst the pickpockets and waiter fraternity in the early hours of the morning. If ever there was a suitable case for mugging – this sailor was it.

When he left the table for a few minutes we all talked about the idea and to John and I it sounded good. Paul and George weren't as keen, as they pointed out the dangers.

'He's a pushover!' John and I persisted. 'All we've got to do after we leave here is to get him in the right place, give him the old one-two and the wallet's ours.' Paul and George weren't really convinced, but grudgingly agreed to join in the venture.

It was around four in the morning when the sailor decided to call it a night and catch a train to bed (we never did find out where). The four of us trooped out into the icy November cold, ostensibly to see him off.

The route led through a couple of car parks and the plan was that we would trip him up in one of them, rough-house him a little, rip open his jacket and lift the wallet. But every time we thought that the moment to strike had arrived something happened to cause a postponement – such as a sudden passer-by appearing – and we would plod on again cheerfully with our intended victim.

As we neared the first likely mugging area Paul and George began to hang back while John and I strode on with the sailor. Then we could hear George complaining that he was feeling tired. The gap between us stretched longer and longer, until finally we heard Paul and George faintly saying 'Tarrah!' They had chickened out and fled for home.

Time was running out when Lennon and I leapt into action pinning the sailor against a car park gate. He knew the name of the game immediately and, despite all the liquor he had taken aboard, he didn't appear to be very drunk as he desperately joined battle. John swung a mean punch at him and knocked him to his knees while I dived in to try to wrestle the wallet free. But it wasn't going to be easy. The seaman, obviously a man of experience, fought back with the tenacity of a man who had probably seen it all before in the seaports of the world, and was soon up on his feet again.

A beefy fist smashed into Lennon, sending him back several feet. Then the sailor started to sling punches my way, but as we grappled in close I somehow managed to grab the wallet. But then, as Lennon dragged himself from the ground, the sailor dived a hand into the rear of his pants and in the dim light of the early hours of a winter's morning we knew that we were looking down the barrel of a gun.

There was no way of telling whether or not it fired bullets or simply gas. And no time to find out. Before we could react his fingers were closing around the trigger, ready to squeeze. Simultaneously, Lennon and I charged at him, heads down, driven forward by sheer instinct rather than any thought of heroics.

We crashed into him as he fired, tumbling him backwards while cartridges flew above us into the night. Both of us lashed out with blow after blow to head and body until we thought he had taken enough punishment to enable us to escape. All we wanted now was to get the hell out of it, and we turned and ran.

Our eyes were already beginning to smart as we sped forward. Fortunately, the gun pumped only gas as the sailor loosed off another four or five shots in our direction. We managed to out-pace the fumes, never looking back, not knowing if he was scrambling to his feet to give chase.

We tore through the streets of Hamburg, scarcely slowing even when there were no tell-tale footsteps to be heard behind us. We had to cover nearly three miles to the Grosse Freiheit and our lungs were almost at

Left: George, Stu and John down at the Hamburg docks. Below: The Reeperbahn, centre of Hamburg's nightclub district.

bursting point when we literally flopped into John's room at the Bambi Kino, where Paul and George were waiting up, eager for news of the mugging and, more important, to hear what share of the loot would be coming their way.

'What'd you get?' George enquired from his bed.

'Not a bloody penny!' Lennon gasped out miserably.

'A bloody nose and a lot of bloody bruises,' I said, equally flatly.

Then I revealed the harrowing story of how, when John and I had hurtled into the sailor as he stood gun in hand, I had dropped the wallet in the mêlée and left it there for him to retrieve. There was no sympathy from the other two Beatles. They simply fell about, choking on their laughter. The Beatles' first – and last – escapade in the hit-and-run world of mugging had proved to be a complete disaster – and we were certain it wasn't over yet, as we took stock of ripped jeans and our lungs slowly returned to normality.

Our eyes still smarted a little from the gas, although that was easy to bear compared with the thoughts of retribution that occupied us now. The sailor was surely not going to forget the four lads from the 'Pool he had wined and dined so generously, who made sweet music but had a pretty lousy way of saying 'Thanks, mate'. We reckoned he would be back, with a boatload of shipmates bent on rending us apart. Lennon and I were petrified as we turned in and I escaped into the darkness of my dungeon. As sleep came my last thoughts were that not only was tomorrow going to be another day, it could well prove to be judgment day, as well.

All the next day, Lennon and I were edgy, looking over our shoulders. On stage we peered through the smoky haze, expecting each minute to glimpse the sailor, teeth bared, waiting to pounce, but he never appeared. No boarding party stormed the Kaiserkeller thirsting for the blood of John Lennon and Pete Best. Perhaps he would show up the following night, but no. Nor the night after that, or any other night.

Gradually our fears diminished and our world returned to near-normality again (life could never really be described as normal in the St Pauli area). Maybe the sailor had had to set sail for some other dangerous port after that eventful night and had been unable to take his revenge. Strangely, in all the time we were in Hamburg, we would never see him again.

It seems tragically ironic that John should eventually meet his death by gunfire nearly twenty years later at the hands of someone he had never met before, let alone tried to harm in any way. In all the four years I knew him I never once heard him talk about death, not even after the frightening confrontation with the sailor. All of us were much more concerned with living and the immediate problems that life always brings. What's more, we were all free from parental and educational reins for the first time and every day was to be enjoyed to the full, even if we sometimes had to worry where our next crust might be coming from.

There was one oasis in this direction. Now that Stu and Astrid were inseparable, the rest of the Beatles became her friends as well and occasionally we visited her home, where we sometimes had a sandwich or a meal prepared by her mother. They appeared to be a comfortably-off family who had indulged Astrid in her pursuit of the arts. Even the decor of her room was a stark study in black and white, down to the black silk sheets on her bed.

Her full name was Astrid Kirchherr and, oddly enough, she had entered our lives through her previous boyfriend, a cultured fellow from Berlin named Klaus Voorman, whose father was a well-known physician. Klaus was another talented artist, who had studied in Hamburg and was now making his way on magazines as an illustrator, designing record sleeves at the same time. He had also taken a course in photography and during his studies had met Astrid, who was working for a photographer and taking pictures herself. This mutual calling brought them closer and when we first met, Klaus had his own room at Astrid's home.

Neither of them were remotely like the usual riff-raff that swarmed into the Reeperbahn each night. Most of the young German clientele were the equivalent of the brawling Teds back home who liked a fight with their music. By contrast, Astrid and Klaus were followers of the French philosophy of existentialism which, according to my dictionary, means 'that a man must create values for himself through action and by living each moment to the full'. When we found out more about this we labelled them 'exis'. They both wore black leather coats, which struck the Beatles as being extremely attractive, and unlike our combed-back style, Klaus wore his hair forward in a fringe on his forehead.

During our residency at the Kaiserkeller, the couple had squabbled one night and Klaus, in a huff, had stalked off alone into St Pauli to try to cheer himself up. As he strolled along the Grosse Freiheit he was suddenly attracted by the din coming from our cellar – although we weren't actually making it at the time. Rory Storm was on stage and we were at a table taking our break between sets.

Klaus sat down next to us. We discovered later he had been drawn to these five Liverpool Teds with their Elvis-style hair and stage suits of funny little grey and white dog-tooth jackets, set off by black shirts and pants and grey winkle-pickers. He thought we looked somewhat ridiculous; we thought we looked the cat's whiskers. However, he did like the music we made when we returned to the stage and during another break tried to start some conversation with us, handing round copies of record sleeves that he had designed. No one made much fuss

UGO HAAS
ANNOVER
20km

of him, although I think Stu, being an artist, showed more interest in the sleeves than the rest of us.

Klaus must have been impressed with us. He returned the following night, again alone, and sat through all our sets, parking himself alongside us once more during the breaks and chatting away in reasonable English. On his third visit he brought Astrid along – not, she told us later, that she had been very enthusiastic about venturing into St Pauli. Nice girls didn't do that kind of thing. She was certainly a striking lady in her black leather jacket contrasting with her short blonde hair and amazingly pallid skin. At 22 she was some three years older than Stu. Somehow she found herself being drawn to us as well and became a regular at our table with Klaus. It soon became clear that, of the five of us, Stu was the main attraction, his eyes still sheltering behind dark shades.

It was love at first sight, Astrid has admitted several times. I never went into this seriously with Stu, but it was obvious that he shared a similar feeling. We all got along fine, even though she knew no English and Klaus had to play interpreter.

Within a short time Astrid was sufficiently a member of the Beatle set to ask us if she could take pictures of us and there followed a remarkable series that has since been published round the world; the Beatles propped against a big dipper background at the Dom (a fairground at the top of the Reeperbahn); spaced among rolling stock at the famous marshalling yards that were an RAF target all through the Second World War; on roofs and in doorways. She made portraits of us with one side of our faces in shadow (her favourite theme of black and white once more) which set a Beatle publicity pattern for years to come.

We all fell in love with Astrid's black leather outfits. Influenced by her, Stu was the first to appear in a black leather jacket. George soon followed suit in a jacket bought off a waiter for £5. Then the rest of us got into line; buying cheap bomber-style models which we wore with the tightest of jeans and cowboy boots. George also discovered the cowboy boots in a shop on the Reeperbahn, creating some envy when he first turned up in a black and white pair. John and I hared off at the earliest opportunity to follow suit; Lennon chose a pair of gold and black, mine were red and black. Paul, who had a reputation amongst the group of watching his pfennigs, stood out for some time but eventually conformed with a black and blue pair. To top off the whole ensemble we bought pink flat caps! These seemed necessities at the time and were primarily intended to be stage outfits, although they became our everyday wear too. No wonder we were becoming poorer by the minute.

During this time Astrid and Stu were getting along like a brush fire. At first she had asked Klaus to teach her enough English to be able to

Previous page: The Beatles photographed by Astrid Kirchherr beside the rollercoaster in the Dom, a fairground near the Reeperbahn.

converse with us, especially Stu. When he succeeded Klaus in her affections she and Stu managed somehow to talk to each other with the aid of a German-English dictionary. Klaus, however, would remain a staunch friend of the Beatles. In the mid-sixties he came to England to be part of a group calling themselves Paddy, Klaus and Gibson (both Paddy and Gibson were Liverpool lads from the group scene), making records on the Pye label but never setting the charts alight. In 1966 he designed the sleeve for the Beatles' album *Revolver* and was also responsible for the decor at the luxury home George Harrison bought in Weybridge, Surrey.

Those signs of success were still a long way into the future as the original Beatles struggled on from day to day in Hamburg with few marks to jingle in their pockets. We were still down, down, down; fed to the teeth with Bruno Koschmieder, with his let-downs and his dictatorial bullying. When we were handed our pittance on Saturdays we would look forward to drinking most of it quickly in an attempt to avoid the bleak realities of life. After finishing on stage we rarely went to bed until the early hours and Sunday morning developed into something of an escape ritual.

Fortified by the night's booze we would sail along to the fish market, a large square down at the waterfront on the banks of the Elbe. We would be laughing and joking, bent on having fun before evening, when we were due back on stage once more, heralding another week on the merry-go-round. At the market we would start by snaffling items from one stall and depositing them on another, causing much confusion which we appreciated even if the owners didn't. What the hell; we were the Beatles out on a Sunday spree and feeling high.

One Sunday – which I will always remember as 'Sunday, Bloody Sunday' – bolder than ever, we took over a knick-knack stall on the quayside, and started giving goods away. A crowd gathered to see the fun, and for a few minutes the stallholder joined in the laughter, taking it all in good humour until the throng thickened and the joke thinned as his trinkets of leather stuff and costume jewelry rapidly began to disappear without even one mark changing hands.

Soon he was playing a series of tugs-of-war with lucky members of the public who didn't want to part with their 'gifts'. When other stallholders, sympathizing, waded in to try to help him retrieve his property, the gathering crowd held them back. Skirmishes flared and swelled, and among those now taking part were some of the inevitable Hamburg waiters – out for the morning and merrily joining the free-for-all with their spring-loaded truncheons.

Within minutes the fighting escalated into a full-scale riot with hundreds of people involved in the scrapping that was mushrooming throughout the market. Pilfering was on a grand scale. Records and record-players disappeared along with pottery, ornaments, paintings, perfumes, food – most of it fish, naturally – all the stuff that one usually finds at open-air markets.

At length the police arrived in strength to pile in with truncheons and lend their own brand of muscle to the scene, which now resembled a battlefield. Taking advantage of the confusion, the Beatles decided to slip across to the hostelry on the waterfront, a favourite spot, where we could sit and drink and observe the turmoil in comfort.

It was like watching a movie – a cast of more than 500 people playing cops and robbers before our very eyes. Somehow we were able to feel detached from the riot we had started and enjoyed the drama that was being enacted in front of us. Bodies were falling around the square and lying where they fell; it reminded us of the Battle of the Alamo. Some people even began to throw fish at each other, which really appealed to the Beatle sense of humour. We creased up in wave after wave of laughter.

When calm was finally restored the police lost little time in seeking us out. 'Bloody Beatles started it!' complained the owner of the stall where we had first played Santa Claus. We stopped laughing when the cops threatened to arrest us. 'It was only meant to be a joke and a bit of a giggle,' we protested. Surely we couldn't be held responsible for *all* the fighting and subsequent thieving. And, we pleaded, we had to be back stage that evening; we couldn't let them down.

The police were surprisingly lenient. We could remain free if we paid so much back in compensation to the stallholders, many of whom had managed to snatch back some of their stolen goods.

However, this was hitting us where it hurt most: we were stony broke. Luckily, as I have said, waiters were a good breed to have on your side. Our friends among them swiftly organized a collection that raised about £50 in reparation. It was enough to solve the problem. The following Sunday we trooped off to the fish market as usual, but this time as very quiet, subdued and well-behaved Beatles. No riot, no skirmishing, nothing untoward: Sunday, quiet bloody Sunday...

Our financial problem, however, was not going to go away. We had to have more money for the work we were doing; we had to have somewhere decent to lay our heads at night and we had now reached the point of no return. We all decided we would have to leave Bruno despite the consequences, however serious they might be.

By this time we had found an ally bearing the unlikely name of Anthony Esmond Sheridan McGinnity. It wasn't the kind of monicker that would fit easily into lights or even to trot around St Pauli. But he had already chopped it down and was calling himself Tony Sheridan, and he would be one more mile-stone along the road to success.

5

RETREAT FROM HAMBURG

Tony Sheridan was from Norwich in Norfolk, which has never earned a reputation as a cradle of rock'n'roll. But there he was in Hamburg, singing and playing guitar and causing something of a stir, a lone East Anglian wolf among the Merseysiders.

Like John Lennon and Stu Sutcliffe, Tony was a former art student who was drawn away from his studies by the lure of rock'n'roll. In the fifties he had journeyed to London to peddle his talent at the celebrated but cramped 2 i's coffee bar in Soho's Old Compton Street, where he began to attract some attention. And there Bruno Koschmieder, on a talent-scouting safari, had found him and enticed him to Hamburg and the Kaiserkeller.

Tony might well have found fame earlier as a member of the Shadows and never entered into the Beatles' lives at all. In the autumn of 1958, as Cliff Richard was about to erupt into stardom with his first record, *Move it*, a guitarist was urgently needed to fill a vacancy in his backing group (then known as the Drifters, later to be renamed the Shadows), to embark on a British variety tour. Cliff's manager of the time, John Foster, had also sallied forth into Soho to keep a date with Tony Sheridan, intent on signing him for the job, but Tony didn't show up. By chance, Foster met a lad there calling himself Hank B. Marvin – and signed him instead, along with his pal Bruce Welch ... Which is the way life goes, I have found; a matter of being in the right place at the right time. For us, at least, Tony happened to be in the right place at the right time – in the comparatively new Top Ten Club, just around the corner from the Grosse Freiheit, on the Reeperbahn itself, and without doubt the smartest and best-conducted rock venue in town.

A year before we arrived in Hamburg the site of the Top Ten was occupied in a small circus sandwiched between two gaudy strip palaces. The main attraction seems to have been topless ladies riding bareback horses round and round the ring. It all sounded a little tame to us compared with what else was on offer in St Pauli, which was also the way a young German named Peter Eckhorn saw the situation when he inherited the place in 1959.

He was only twenty years old and had already been fired by the tremendous advance of rock'n'roll and its adoption by millions of young people throughout the western world. He had also noted with much interest the thriving business rock was doing at the Kaiserkeller. Wasting little time, Eckhorn gutted the premises of the old circus, sent the nags and the nudes packing and transformed it into a modern club, calling it the Top Ten. He, too, had flown off to England to survey the rock scene and scout for talent. For some reason young Germans seemed incapable of making this music for themselves; rock'n'roll was after all an American invention which was easier for their English-speaking counterparts in Britain to mimic than for Germans, with their strong tradition of oom-pah music and hearty lyrics.

'I felt rock was the thing to give our youth,' Peter told us when we got to know him. 'They were hearing records of rock and beat music, but not getting enough of it in live form.'

By the time we were installed in the Grosse Freiheit, Eckhorn had already enticed Tony Sheridan away from Bruno to the Top Ten, the never-failing carrot being more money plus more pleasant surroundings. This then was where we found him, resident star and packing 'em in. He was nineteen.

He became an immediate friend of the Beatles and introduced us to Eckhorn, who struck us at once as being an affable chap who knew where he was going and was only a few years older than we were. The whole set-up at the Top Ten attracted us. The main room was large with a low-slung black ceiling and could accommodate 1,500 to 2,000 young people a night. Tony bedded down in a small dormitory upstairs which, even if it wasn't knee-deep in pile carpet, I likened to Liverpool's four-star Adelphi Hotel compared with our dismal pits behind the cinema.

After some four months' slaving away at the two venues in the Grosse Freiheit, our crowd-pulling reputation had become known along the length of the Reeperbahn, a fact that had already impressed Peter Eckhorn. 'Why don't you come and play for me?' he asked us one night when we nipped into the club during our break. 'You will be welcome any time.' He added that he would pay us something like £1 a day more as well, which would mean another seven quid a week in our pockets. It was an offer we couldn't resist and we decided that we would have to give Bruno a final ultimatum – more money or we quit. We still only had a verbal contract at the Kaiserkeller so to hell with the consequences; he hadn't kept his word either.

The problem was how to tell Bruno without causing a riot? We didn't have to, it transpired. He had already received reports of our intended defection from his personal spy – George Sterner, the waiter who had packed into Allan Williams' mini-bus with us on the journey from England. We had originally thought Herr Sterner was 'one of the boys', but as soon as we arrived in Hamburg his attitude had changed. He was a powerfully-built man, and I had frequently seen him picking on smaller victims. Apart from being one of Bruno's top waiters he also acted as his translator and go-between with the Beatles. He kept tabs on us for his master but at the same time carried on a pretence of being our buddy.

It was a fuming Koschmieder who called us together and we needed no interpreter to translate his rage and his refusal to pay us more. Anyway Paul and I had by this time become pretty fluent in German ourselves. The threats came out like bursts from a machine-gun. 'You'll be shot!' he stormed. Whether or not he meant that literally, it was certainly a threat to be taken seriously. He was surrounded by his own gang of plug-uglies, always at hand with coshes and flick-knives.

'If you leave me you won't ever play the Top Ten!' he said menacingly. 'You can take that any way you like. My boys know how to create trouble!'

At the very least, he promised, we 'would end up with broken fingers!' His lads, as we well knew, would also find no problem in breaking anyone's legs at his behest. These were risks we had to run, but we felt that even Bruno wouldn't be crazy enough to send us back to Liverpool in a coffin.

By this time we were as angry as he was. When he stood four-square against our ultimatum, Lennon barked at him fiercely: 'Get stuffed! We're off to the Top Ten!' There would be no going back for us now: the gloves were off. Those final days at the Kaiserkeller were eventful. First of all, I managed to even the score with the spying George Sterner. It was late one afternoon during a rehearsal at the Kaiserkeller – it was closed in the afternoons – and we had taken two girls along with us. There was the usual clowning around – watched with interest by Sterner. Then the girls fancied a dance and I started to jive with one of them. For some reason Sterner didn't like this at all.

'No dancing!' he ordered, pushing and shoving into us.

'Look!' I snapped at him, 'what we do in our free time has nothing to do with you!'

He slapped the other girl as she began to make her way out and I exploded: 'You're a bloody nancy boy!' I went on to accuse him of tale-telling to Bruno when all the time 'you're supposed to be our friend. C'mon – let's have a go!' A showdown had been inevitable and if it hadn't been with me it would have been with one of the others. I flattened him – for which Bruno lopped £5 off the pay due to me. The other Beatles were each fined £5 for 'baiting' Sterner.

After the fracas with Sterner, the cops suddenly took an interest in

George Harrison, discovering that he was still only seventeen. They ordered him home to Liverpool immediately for being under age in St Pauli. He left us sadly, like some little-boy-lost, and we had a very strong feeling that after all this time somebody must have tipped off the police.

But still nothing would stop us moving on to the Top Ten for we still made a foursome with the faithful Stu. The three of us who were left planned to move as secretly as possible from the Bambi Kino. Lennon was the first to gather up his kit and personal belongings and set off for the new abode just a short walk away on the Reeperbahn. He made it in one piece and in the top floor dormitory we would share with Tony Sheridan he claimed the bottom bed of a two-tier bunk.

For Paul and I, moving proved to be a more difficult chore, as we had to scramble our goods and chattels together in the pitch darkness of the windowless dungeons. In desperation we invented a novel method of illumination to help us see to pack. We pinned four rubber contraceptives to the frayed tapestry on the corridor wall outside our doors. The condoms spluttered and flickered and gave off a vile smell, but at least we had a little light. By the time we made our exit through the pit of the cinema the condoms had almost burned out, having scorched and briefly singed some of the rotting material on the wall.

Safely reunited with Lennon in the Top Ten dormitory, we felt something like prisoners of war who had tunnelled their way to freedom. We smoked and laughed and generally agreed that Bruno could kiss-my-ass. John was already comfortably installed. Paul elected to take the top deck above him and I booked a bottom pit on another two-decker bunk. Tony Sheridan, perched on another top bunk, was there to help the convivial atmosphere along. The dormitory was bright and airy and there were even windows! For Paul and I it was a new world.

When we took the stage downstairs for our Top Ten opening the same happy mood prevailed as we 'made show', boozed, laughed and basked in the applause. Among the crowd we noted some Beatle devotees who had decided to move from the Kaiserkeller along with us, but, as the hours drifted by, there was no sign of an invasion by Koschmieder's Klan, intent on breaking our heads or fingers or both. There was still time, we knew – but Bruno had threatened that we would *never* play the Top Ten. Perhaps the fact that Peter Eckhorn also employed a sizeable posse of typical Hamburg waiters, equally able to dish out their own brand of hard knocks, was too much of a deterrent. As we settled in, we felt that at last we were getting somewhere: a good venue, better wages, pleasant living quarters. But it wouldn't last for long.

The quiet solitude of our dormitory was harshly disturbed around 5.30 am during our second night there. We hadn't been in bed an hour or so after the long, arduous night's work when the bliss of deep sleep was abruptly invaded by shouts.

'Paul McCartney! Pete Best!' two voices were yelling.

I rubbed my eyes open and blinked. The lights had been switched on and two men were yanking Paul off his top bunk. They looked like cops, and soon made it clear that they were; plain-clothes cops, big and wide of shoulder.

Paul was still coming to while they hauled me out on to the floor. Lennon raised his head, only half-awake, and sleepily wanted to know 'What's going on?' before slumping back into oblivion. Tony Sheridan stirred but slept on.

'Get dressed!' one of the gorilla-like cops growled.

During those breadline days pyjamas were a luxury beyond our reach and we all slept in our underpants. 'Get dressed!' came the call again. Impatiently, the two policeman pulled and tugged at us as we tried to hitch up our jeans. We were still trying to squeeze our feet into our cowboy boots when they began to drag us down the stairs.

It was now early December and an icy winter's morning greeted us as the plain-clothes men bundled us towards a police car waiting at the kerbside. Whatever was happening to Paul and I – and it was plain that John was not going to be included – seemed to have an air of finality about it. We started to protest about the cold and pleaded for time to collect more clothing. Reluctantly the policemen allowed us to wrap up a little more against the biting wind and to stuff a few personal bits and pieces into our pockets. Downstairs once more we were herded into the car like a couple of bank robbers and whisked off to a police station along the Reeperbahn.

We were roughly escorted inside and dumped on a bench, where we languished for half an hour, the silence punctured only by repeated guttural snarls of 'Bambi Kino fire!' from one of them. Paul and I decided to play dumb and innocent. A scorched patch of ancient tapestry could never add up to a blaze.

At last a station policeman, whom we assumed to be a more senior officer, took us to a barren room lit only by a naked bulb. For well over an hour he grilled us with question after question concerning 'a fire at the Bambi Kino'. Perhaps the interrogation wouldn't have taken so long if his knowledge of English had been a little more extensive. But the message came through loud as well as clear: he had no doubt that we were responsible.

'I am now going to charge you with setting fire to the cinema', he concluded, revealing that our accuser was one Bruno Koschmieder, which scarcely surprised us. But our earlier nonchalance was gone. Both Paul and I were rapidly becoming very worried as the seriousness of the situation hit us. There had to be some way out – after all we weren't German nationals; they couldn't do this to us. There was one slender hope.

'Can we ring the British Consul?' I asked.

'No phone calls,' the officer said firmly.

Despite the near-Arctic weather outside we began to sweat a little when a police surgeon arrived. We peeled off to the waist for a brief examination and coughed a couple of times for him. Then we were formerly charged with arson, after which the officer lightened our gloom by announcing that the proceedings were over and that we would be going.

The two plain-clothes men reappeared and hustled us once more into the police car. Ah, well, we thought, back to our billet, our warm beds and all that sleep we needed to catch up on. Our relief was short-lived. 'This is not the way to the Top Ten!' Paul suddenly cried out, peering at the unfamiliar scenery through the car windows. Instead it was the way to Hamburg's main prison with its great brick walls and sombre double iron gates. A prison officer opened a grille in a door and enough of him was visible to glimpse the gun at his shoulder.

The gates swung open and the car nosed through, followed by the sinister clang as they were shut behind us, a mournful signal that we were now cut off from the rest of civilization. At reception – for want of a better word – they relieved us of our belts and jackets. We weren't even going to be given the chance of committing suicide. Then we were frog-marched along stark corridors, past cells with ominous bars and men in prison garb.

We eventually fetched up in a cell on the third floor of this fortress of a jail, furnished simply with two bunk beds. There was only one opening apart from the door – a grille which let in the cold air some nine feet up one of the walls. The door was locked on us and we were left alone.

Paul and I felt absolutely shattered. This had to be the end of the road. Jail! If the Beatles had any future at this particular moment it looked distinctly black. Feeling utterly hopeless, we flopped on to the beds, whacked. But there was going to be no rest or any escape from the dread of reality by sleeping.

The cell door opened and in came a prison officer waving a pistol. 'No lying on the bed!' he ordered gruffly. 'You must sit,' gesturing with his gun. 'Feet on the ground! Keep your hands on the side of the beds!'

We did as we were told and he let himself out and locked us in once more. We sat there like a couple of dummies and the minutes dawdled by with nothing to accompany them but silence and despair.

After an hour or so the monotony and the cramp began to get to us and we adventurously climbed on to the top of a bunk to have a look at the world outside the high grille. Prisoners were at exercise in the courtyard below, walking aimlessly round and round, and we took in the scene with little enthusiasm. Perhaps we might be joining them sometime in the not too distant future.

We must have been cooped up for around three hours when the lock turned in the door to admit the two gorillas who had originally broken into our hard-earned sleep at the Top Ten. Once again there was the indignity of being frog-marched to the front of the jail, where we were given back our jackets and belts. Then we were bustled once more into the police car.

When we moved off it didn't take long to realize that this wasn't the route to the Top Ten either. We were on our way to the airport. 'Why?' we both asked, but no one was willing to answer the question just yet. It was only after our arrival in the airport lounge that one of the gorillas spoke. 'You're going back to England,' he announced at long last while passengers stared at the two scruffs, now badly in need of a shave, being hustled along by two brawny men.

'But we've got no passports, no kit, no money except for a handful of coins!' we both protested vigorously.

They had taken meticulous care of the administration. While we had been experiencing a nasty taste of jail they had returned to the Top Ten and searched through our kit and unearthed our passports – but these were all they had brought with them. It was a vivid demonstration of what Germany could do to people it considered to be undesirable. 'You're going home, courtesy of the German Government,' one of the gorillas said smugly. 'And you can never come back to Germany again!'

At that moment Paul made a sudden break from our escort to a telephone kiosk. I squeezed in after him and planted myself between him and the door, determined to keep out the gorillas jostling around outside and now growing irritable with a gathering crowd of interested onlookers. McCartney found enough coins in his pockets to make a frantic call to the British Consul and he garbled out our story. But the consul, sympathetic though he was, explained that there was nothing that he could possibly do at the present moment. We would have to fly home as the Germans bid and then file any protest from there.

The gorillas finally managed to open the door and pull us out. There wasn't even time to replace the receiver, which Paul left dangling. They even frog-marched us to the boarding gate, and one of them accompanied us to the foot of the steps up to the plane. A stewardess was told the grisly tale and given our passports.

We sat in our seats, feeling like a couple of very tired criminals, which, no doubt, was how some of the passengers must have seen us. At least there was one bright spot – a meal to ease the hunger that had built up through the trials of the day.

It was late afternoon by the time the aircraft touched down at

Heathrow Airport. Our passports were returned to us and we cleared Customs with absolutely nothing to declare and no luggage to be searched, since most of what we owned was still at the Top Ten Club in Hamburg. All the money we could muster between us was about 15 shillings (75 pence) and much of that was in pfennigs, which we managed to change at the airport bank. An airline coach took us to the West London Air Terminal and from there we made our own way to Euston Station, leaving us almost broke in the gathering dusk.

We called home, transferring the charges; Paul phoned his father, I rang Mo. They listened to the dismal story of our deportation and hurried off to wire money to us at Euston's Post Office so that we could buy our train tickets to Liverpool. There was another long wait for the money to come through, during which we spent what little cash we had left on cups of tea and coffee in the station buffet. We finally caught the last Liverpool train, one that stopped everywhere, and it was about two in the morning when it shuffled into Lime Street Station and expired with a hiss of steam. Exhausted and cold, and scarcely able to speak, Paul and I each took a taxi to our respective homes – where they had to be paid off by our parents.

Mo was surprised and shocked when she saw me standing at the door at Number Eight Hayman's Green.

'What an object of art!' she exclaimed, surveying me in the light from the hallway as I stood dejectedly in leather jacket, scuffed jeans and cowboy boots. Then I had to ask her for the four-mile cab fare. When I told her the full story afterwards she began to get worried. 'This means you'll never get back to Germany again,' she said. Today she recalls: 'I was also worried that the case might not just end with deportation and that the police would be calling at Number Eight,' which wouldn't have pleased her at all. She remembers too that I 'looked thinner than when I went away – a real figure of despair!'

LIME STREET STATION
1 to 6
7 to 11
SBU 599
KEEP LEFT

Pete back behind the drums in Liverpool.

6

PICKING UP THE PIECES

Fate continued to play a pretty grim hand against the Beatles. December in Liverpool was decidely bleak and not just because of the winter weather. For days following our unceremonious booting out by the German authorities there was no contact between Paul and I, or with George.

Paul signed on at the Labour Exchange and landed a job as a lorry driver's mate, I believe. Lennon lingered on in Germany and followed us home about a week later, heartily homesick so he told me when we were eventually reunited. Like Paul and me, he had arrived back in the early hours and had to wake his Aunt Mimi by throwing stones at her bedroom window. Stu stayed on at Astrid's place and would not return until 1961 was well into its stride in the coming January.

The future of the Beatles seemed to concern me more than the others. It was obvious that there wouldn't be one at all if we didn't make some effort to retrieve the kit we had been forced to leave behind at the Top Ten. John had staggered home with his guitar across his shoulder, but Paul's was still in Hamburg, stranded there with my shining mother-of-pearl drums, and I wondered if we would ever see them again.

Mo and I went into action and made some frantic phone calls to Peter Eckhorn. He was extremely sympathetic and promised to get the stuff back to us by sea as soon as possible. He was a man of his word. Within days he called me to say that the kit had been crated and that the freight invoice would be in the mail. On the day of the ship's arrival in Liverpool, Mo and I booked a taxi – there was no family car at the time – and headed off to the Customs shed at Dingle.

The crate was massive and would never fit into a cab, so Mother and I set to work on the wharfside and broke it down. Drums, guitar, sound equipment, personal gear – we piled the lot into the taxi and left the debris on the dock. This was the first hurdle cleared, thanks to Peter Eckhorn, and I began to feel a little more optimistic. (Needless to say we never had any word from the German authorities, nor did we really expect it. After all, we had originally entered Germany under false pretences, and as far as the German cops were concerned Paul and I were arsonists.) And the smell of burning had followed us from Hamburg as well.

Inspired by the sight of more than a thousand young Germans converging nightly on the bright new Top Ten Club, Allan Williams, on his return, had decided to set up a club on similar lines during our absence and call it, too, the Top Ten. This would be *the* place for the rock fraternity on Merseyside. And the Beatles would be the resident group.

Sadly it was not to be. Within a week of opening in early December – about the time we were defecting from the Kaiserkeller – the place was a smouldering shell. How the fire started which destroyed the club is still a mystery, but there has always been a suspicion of arson. It was a shattering blow for Allan – and for us when we heard the news, for it deprived us of a ready-made showcase for our talents. We would really have to pick up the pieces now if we hoped to get anywhere.

I sometimes think that the whole Beatles' saga might well have been different if Allan's Top Ten Club had escaped the flames. We would probably have stayed with him in what would undoubtedly have become Liverpool's Number One rock spot. Having a manager around us all the time – a man already interested in the booming record scene – there would have been little likelihood of Brian Epstein coming in search of a disc we would make in Hamburg and subsequently wanting to take us under his wing and to change us into nice, clean boy-next-door types.

It is arguable that Ringo Starr might never have been called in to replace me, because the big break on records at Parlophone – flashpoint of my being ousted, as we shall see – might have eluded us. As Allan himself said in 1980: 'Brian Epstein was probably the best thing that ever happened to the Beatles. They reached greater heights than they probably would have done with me.

'He was part of them. His determination and dedication got them to the top. I possibly didn't have the perseverance. But I was the acorn from which they grew and I was part of an exciting decade and no one can take that away from me.'

When Allan did part with the Beatles to Epstein around the close of 1961 he literally gave us away and no transfer fee took place. 'You can have them,' he told Brian Epstein, 'but if I were you I wouldn't touch them with a bargepole!'

Allan, however, played no part at all in our regrouping as 1960 drew to a close and he would show little or no interest in us until much later when we were really established – and from his point of view, too late.

John, Paul, George and I got together at last during the latter half of

December, 1960, and set about rebuilding the Beatles, gradually regaining some of our old confidence. Oddly, it was George and I who made the first moves, running around town in search of venues to play – without success, I must report. But the Casbah was still thriving and Mo cheerfully threw us a lifeline with a booking shortly before Christmas. She ordered a large poster billing us as the 'Fabulous Beatles!' – the birth of a description that would long endure. She also included us in a local dance-date promotion. The success of the Casbah had led to other promoters hiring halls and booking groups that appeared there – a signal for Mo to say: 'Why don't we go out and put on our own promotions?' This she began to do, again successfully, and tickets would go on sale at the Casbah.

It was a new-look Casbah. While we were in Germany three rooms had been knocked into one large one away from the jukebox, giving much more space for the groups to perform and for members to crowd in to watch them.

Here we introduced a new although temporary Beatle that the rest of the world seems never to have known existed. He was a chemistry student name Chas Newby and he had played guitar in my old group, the Blackjacks, before I left to take the trail to Hamburg. Now we co-opted him into the Beatle fold on the understanding that Stu would replace him if and when he returned from Hamburg. By coincidence, Chas was left-handed – like Paul McCartney, who would eventually take Stu's place on bass guitar. We could only acquire a right-handed guitar for Chas, which he had to play backwards.

We introduced a British audience for the first time to 'making show' in the cellars beneath my home, clowning and leaping and doing most of the things that Bruno Koschmieder had demanded when we made our German debut at the Indra Club. None of the noisy madness was lost on the Casbah crowd; they shouted and stamped their feet along with us. Girls screamed and afterwards descended on us for autographs. It was a taste of things to come; the spark that kindled Beatlemania.

Chas Newby joined in wholeheartedly, quickly adjusting himself to this Beatle bedlam and was absolutely amazed at the fever we created among the audience. 'It was just like the movies,' he recalled when I met him in Liverpool many years later during the preparation of this book. He now lives in Birmingham and is in industrial management, but will never forget his days as a stand-in Beatle.

'I remember them vividly,' he said. 'It used to make my feet ache with all the stamping we had to put into the act, but I loved every minute.'

Chas played some half-dozen dates with us and took part in the memorable appearance at Merseyside's Litherland Town Hall on 27th December 1960 – a performance that is generally considered to have been the blast-off date of Beatlemania, as audience reaction would come to be labelled.

We were billed as being 'direct from Hamburg', which led some of the new-found fans to believe that we were German when they besieged us after the show. No doubt the leather jackets and outrageous cowboy boots into which we tucked our jeans were partly responsible. Some of the autograph seekers even complimented us on our good knowledge of English when we said a few grateful words as we scrawled our signatures in their books. Litherland was an explosion in the fortunes of the Beatles. We were playing for dancing in a hall that could accommodate some 1,500 on the floor at one time, but they stopped dancing when we played and surged forward in a crowd to be nearer to us, to watch every movement and above all to scream. People didn't go to a dance to scream: this was news! It had happened at the Casbah; now it was happening in Litherland. The magic of the Beatles was busting out. Nothing like it happened to the two nondescript groups who shared the evening as supporting bill.

The fee for that night was a princely £6, which gave us a pound each, the sixth share going to Frank Garner, whom Mo employed as a bouncer at the Casbah, but who acted as our driver that night and humped the kit.

The all-important Litherland date came to us by courtesy of a fellow named Bob Wooler, a railway clerk who had given up his job to front Allan Williams' ill-fated Top Ten Club – and one more name to add to the catalogue of people who would become a major influence in the eruption of the Beatles upon the world. Bob, a man with a neat line in pop patter, had already been collecting something of a following himself on Merseyside as a disc jockey and dancehall MC. After the Top Ten fire he found a new niche with promoter Brian Kelly, the man who booked us for Litherland.

The Litherland inside story was revealed some time later in *Mersey Beat*, Liverpool's own music bi-weekly, founded and edited in the summer of 1961 by Bill Harry, another old boy of the College of Art, where he had been a friend of Stu Sutcliffe and had also known John Lennon. The article, a series of quotes by Kelly, was headlined across three columns: THE MAN WHO DISCOVERED THE BEATLES. Several people would make the same claim, but *Mersey Beat* did acknowledge, in the introduction published in the issue dated June 20–July 4, 1963, that Brian Kelly was the first promoter 'to really have faith in the group, and their early appearances at Litherland Town Hall marked a major turning point in their career.' (However, I always reckon that Mo was really the first!) Kelly disclosed that he had been short of a group for this landmark occasion at Litherland – and only a chance telephone call from Bob Wooler on Christmas Day saved the situation. Mr Kelly went on: 'Bob Wooler said "I've found a group for you at the Jacaranda [we

The start of Beatlemania.

LITHERLAND
TOWN HALL
EVERY THURSDAY
THE MAGNIFICENT
BEATLES ! !
JOHN, PAUL, GEORGE AND
PETE
ALWAYS A
LIVELY
LITHERLAND TIME TOWN HERE HALL
YOUR THURSDAY DANCE DATE

weren't playing there, simply sitting around idling our time] and they're free. They want £8. Will they do?"

'"Not at that price, they won't," I said. "A group won't increase my attendance enough to warrant that..." We finally agreed to pay them £6.'

'On their first appearance I was completely knocked out by them. They had a pounding, pulsating beat which I knew would be big box office. When they had finished playing I posted some bouncers on the door of their dressing room to prevent other promoters in the hall from entering. I went inside and booked them solidly for months ahead.'

Wooler himself described the Litherland engagement as having been a 'fantastic night' in an article he wrote for *Mersey Beat* (issue dated August 31–September 14, 1961). Asked to explain our sudden leap in popularity, he wrote that it was mainly because we had 'resurrected original style rock'n'roll music, the origins of which are to be found in American Negro singers'. We had 'hit the scene when it had been emasculated by figures like Cliff Richard and sounds like those electronic wonders, the Shadows and their many imitators. Gone was the drive that inflamed the emotions...'

'In the Beatles,' he felt, 'was the stuff that screams are made of.' And he described us as 'human dynamos generating a beat which was irresistible'. He thought we were 'musically authoritative and physically magnetic, example the mean, moody magnificence of drummer Pete Best – a sort of teenage Jeff Chandler...'

These were magnificent words of Wooler's and a remarkable summing up – and music to our ears, of course (though he didn't mention the other Beatles by name). I was, however, far from being moody, but I admit that I probably didn't smile as much as the others did, although I was seldom conscious of this while pounding out the beat. Captive behind the drums, I was unable to indulge myself in crazy antics like John and Paul, and I did have a habit of looking down while I played, which might have been wrongly interpreted as moodiness or shyness. I wasn't all that shy, either, but perhaps I had to take the job a little more seriously, as did George Harrison in those embryo days. What was obvious was that the girls were paying me a whole lot of attention – whether I smiled or not.

Along with the rest of the group I was also receiving some unwelcome attention from lads who reckoned (not without reason) that the Beatles were stealing their girlfriends. Scraps were commonplace and impossible to avoid as our fame began to spread after Litherland. Any time we dived into a pub or a bar for a drink we were liable to be picked upon. Teds bemoaning the loss of their girls sought us out wherever we were appearing, although the violence at home was nothing compared with the brutality in Hamburg whenever the waiters waded in.

When Stu rejoined us on Merseyside halfway through January, he was always a target because of his small stature. George, who was not much bigger, also had to be rescued by a couple of bouncers from what promised to be a serious beating-up on one occasion at the Aintree Institute. The more robust Lennon was always ready to have a go, and usually I had a go at his side. John and I became a sort of rescue squad for Stu. One night at Lathom Hall, which became a regular venue for us after the Litherland triumph, Stu was jumped on by a bunch of thugs and was taking considerable punishment when two girl fans breathlessly dashed up to us with the news.

Lathom Hall was a two-tier dance hall in a tough area and the Teds had been able to trap Stu backstage. John and I doubled back and in usual style put our heads down and charged into the fray, freeing Stu and collecting our fair share of knocks along the way. Lennon broke a finger belting a Ted and had to play guitar for a while wearing a splint.

Down in the city the music that filtered out into Mathew Street from the bricklined tunnels that comprised the Cavern Club at Number 10 was still mostly traditional jazz. But in that January of 1961, as the five of us joined forces once more, there was a small move by the Cavern management to incorporate some of this new-fangled Mersey Beat that was continuing to sprout up around the city. Bob Wooler began a lunchtime residency as a DJ in this damp and sweltering sewer of a venue, bringing in a new audience of youngsters to dance or listen to current disc offerings. Many of them took their sandwiches along with them. At around the same time, Mo called Ray McFall, the Cavern's proprietor, and tried to sell him on the idea of more live rock'n'roll. She told him firmly that he would be doing himself a great favour by booking a group calling themselves the Beatles.

Bob Wooler, who had been greatly impressed by our showing at Litherland, began to pester McFall as well about these scruffs in cowboy boots trading as the Beatles. At last McFall gave the nod and we moved into the Cavern for the first time to perform at lunchtime, while jazz continued to reign supreme at night. It was one more milestone – and we took sandwiches as well to scoff between numbers.

Much of our lives, it seemed, was destined to be spent underground. First the Casbah; then the Indra and the Kaiserkeller in Hamburg; and now the Cavern, which was aptly named. Only Peter Eckhorn's Top Ten Club had had us playing at street level!

Mathew Street was made up of tall, gaunt buildings that were or had been fruit and vegetable warehouses, a narrow little street that had a character and a tang of its own. The Cavern's tiny stage was at the end of a tunnel, flanked by two other tunnels with archways; offstage there was a sweatbox of a bandroom. Fresh air was the one commodity the Cavern

CAVERN

was really short on. The kids, who soon began to queue to see the Beatles, spent their lunch-breaks in a self-induced steam bath; a body dropping to the floor in a faint was a regular sight that caused little stir. After ten minutes of thrashing away on stage our hair would be stuck to our heads with perspiration and beads of sweat would run down our cheeks and necks. Even the ceilings dripped with a mixture of condensation and peeling paint that we dubbed 'Liverpool dandruff'. The whole place – and the people who either danced or played there – used to reek of the disinfectant that of necessity was liberally sprayed around. You could always tell a Cavern fan when you met one away from the club – the aroma lingered.

We were paid £5 between us for those early Cavern dates – and quite a sizeable proportion of it crossed the counter of the Grapes, the little pub in Mathew Street that became an oasis for the sweltering Beatles in this desert of fruit, veg and disinfectant.

As the weeks hurried by with their round of dance hall dates, Cavern lunchtimes and increasing recognition, we often talked of our Hamburg days and began to feel the tug of that lively city. We all found that we were missing St Pauli, despite the sad and sordid end to our first tour there. Stu, we discovered, had also been requested to leave by the authorities, but there had been none of the unpleasantness that Paul and I had to endure. Now Stu, even more than the rest of us, wished to return to be reunited with Astrid, with whom he was still very much in love. We remembered how friendly Peter Eckhorn had been and the pleasantness of his Top Ten Club; his words that we would always be welcome there kept coming back into our minds. But there was still an arson charge outstanding against McCartney and myself, as far as we knew, and we recalled the boast of the German cop that we would never again set foot in the country.

Paul and I decided to try and do something about having the slate wiped clean. We wrote to the immigration authorities in Hamburg and called on the German Consul in Liverpool, pouring out our tale of woe. At the other end, Peter Eckhorn, who was to prove a real brick, played his part and was able to confirm (at least to us) that the only damage we had caused to the Bambi Kino was the scorching of a frayed piece of tapestry.

Koschmieder, we learned, withdrew the charge. Whether or not Bruno suffered an attack of conscience we never did find out, but on the face of it there was no charge to answer anyway. Four spluttering condoms were not exactly a conflagration. Paul went on record later as saying: 'We couldn't have burned the place if we had gallons of petrol – it was made of stone.'

What was more important, it transpired, was that we never did have the right credentials to enter the country to work on that first visit. Allan

Previous page, left: Pete at the Cavern Club. Right top: The Beatles on stage at a lunchtime session at the Cavern. Below: George, Pete, John and Paul relax between sets outside the Cavern in Mathew Street.

Williams had 'talked' us into Germany, but it could never happen that way again. The Consul in Liverpool lent a kindly ear. He even broke into a laugh when he gave us the glad news that we were free men again and could return to Germany without any fears of reprisal. 'But this time,' he grinned, 'you go with visas and work permits!' To cap it all, on February 25th George Harrison celebrated his eighteenth birthday and could now work in St Pauli without fear of the cops putting a hand on his collar.

By this time I had more or less become acting manager of the Beatles, lumbering myself with all the paper work and attention to details. The rest of the group just let me get on with it and Allan Williams gradually faded from our scene.

I had rung Peter Eckhorn at the Top Ten to remind him that he had said a welcome would always be awaiting us. As ever, he was a man who kept a promise, and invited us to go back in the coming April. Tony Sheridan, he said, was still in residence and would be appearing with us. It was good news which was greeted by the Beatles with wide smiles.

Shortly before we embarked on our second invasion of Hamburg, we were to suffer what I still recall as our Aldershot nightmare. This Hampshire town, with its well known military background, sounded like some far-flung outpost to us. Apart from Hamburg, we had spent most of our time working on Merseyside, where now we could always be sure to pull a crowd and have the birds screaming. Thus Aldershot was pasture new, promising new faces and, we hoped, new fans.

The promoter who booked us in March for this latest adventure was a Liverpudlian named Sam Leach. He laid on a mini-bus for the occasion with the words THE FAB BEATLES emblazoned on its sides. En route we were all laughing and clowning and looking forward to a rapturous welcome from a sea of expectant youngsters on our first out-of-town British engagement. But once we arrived, our laughter soon subsided. The venue looked like an ex-army bomb shelter and there were no posters on the doors proclaiming our talents. Sam didn't appear to worry. 'The people in Aldershot know you're coming,' he said confidently.

At 7.30 the doors were opened to let the crowds in. There were no crowds. There was nobody at all.

'You sure you got the date right, Sam?' I asked. He nodded, still not very much concerned.

By 8.30 there was a crowd of six. They were all fellows, propping up the walls. 'Don't worry, lads,' Sam assured us after our first set on stage had failed to inject some life into the doomy atmosphere. 'Have a drink,' he said cheerfully, which we proceeded to do from the crates of brown he had provided.

The customers slowly swelled to a total of ten and then a dozen. Only two of them were girls. There was only one answer – act the goat perhaps a little more than usual. Half way through one number George and John put on their overcoats and took to the floor to dance a foxtrot together while the rest of us struggled along making enough music for them and the handful of spectators (you couldn't really call them an audience).

We clowned our way through the whole of the second half. John and Paul deliberately played wrong chords and added words to the songs that were never in the original lyrics. We even sang sea shanties. What the customers thought we never knew but, damn it, we were going to enjoy ourselves even if they weren't, despite the fact that they had paid something like three shillings and sixpence each for their evening's entertainment – a lot of money in those days. When it mercifully came to an end a crestfallen Sam gave us the dread news: 'I'm sorry,' he said, 'but I haven't got enough cash to pay you for the gig.'

'You'd better get hold of some,' we all told him.

He scraped together £12 – when we should have been receiving £20. We ignored him in the mini-bus on the way back to Liverpool, treating him to one of our Beatle Silences, which could be quite frosty, with solemn, sour faces gazing vacantly into space.

Sam kept out of our way for some nine months after that fiasco. And we never did collect the rest of the money – at least I didn't.

Above: The Aldershot gig – the Beatles' only failure. Right: John and George relieve the boredom at Aldershot by fox-trotting round the Queen's Hall.

BIG BEAT SESSIONS
AT
THE PALAIS BALLROOM
ALDERSHOT
EVERY SATURDAY
commencing this Saturday
9th DECEMBER
Presenting a "Battle of the Bands"
LIVERPOOL v LONDON
LIVERPOOL'S No. "1" BAND
Direct from Their German Tour
THE BEATLES
VERSUS
IVOR JAY & the JAYWALKERS
Plus Two Other Star Groups
7-30 p.m. to 11-30 p.m.
BAR
BUFFET
ADMISSION 5/-

The Beatles back in Hamburg – this time at the Top Ten Club.

7

THE BEATLES BUILD IT UP

St Pauli hadn't changed. It was April, the Reeperbahn was as busy as ever, and we were greeted by springtime smiles from all the familiar old faces. We had travelled to Hamburg by train and boat, manhandling all the gear ourselves along the way, Astrid was at the station to meet Stu and the rest of us. She was wearing a stunning black leather trouser suit, which fascinated us all; the pants were real eye-catchers – and trend setters for the Beatles, as it would transpire.

There were hearty handshakes at the Top Ten from Peter Eckhorn and Tony Sheridan, now a Hamburg veteran. There was another Kaiserkeller defector at the club as well, a tough little guy named Horst Fascher, who had been one of Koschmieder's prominent henchmen but had thrown in his lot to become an aide to Eckhorn. And surprise, surprise – dear old Mutti, the lavatory lady, had also crossed over to the Top Ten.

The atmosphere was in marked contrast to the gloom and disappointment of our first arrival. Upstairs we laid claim to our bunk beds, George Harrison moving in above me on the top deck. This would be our much improved home almost until July, for Peter had the dormitory enlarged to give us more space and had even put in a bath. Four of us took up residence there with Tony while Stu returned to Astrid's house.

Predictably, Stu was the first Beatle into leather trousers; Astrid and he must have been one of the earliest unisex couples on the fashion scene. They even had matching pale complexions. It wasn't all that long – as soon as we could afford it, in fact – before the rest of the Beatles were draping their legs in black leather and looking for longer jackets to replace the bomber-style models now showing signs of wear. Our gear, however, was strictly downmarket compared with Astrid and Stu's.

I was the first to buy a longer leather coat in a shop at the end of the Grosse Freheit. When Lennon saw it he could hardly wait to follow suit. 'Great!' he exclaimed. 'Where'd you get it? How much?'

It had cost about £15. Next day he collected his marks together and got into line. George joined in the new look as well but Paul had yet to make a move. (Paul was always rather careful with money – while the rest of us always passed our cigarettes round, he would frequently sneak one of his own to himself.

There was only one thing to do. We all paraded in front of him and told him it was now up to him to buy a longer coat. 'This is our new image,' it was impressed on him, but he still wasn't keen. In the end we had to escort him to the shop. 'This guy wants a coat like ours,' the assistant was told. 'Size 38–40!'

Paul would be the target of some good-natured ribbing about being a bit of a meanie – sometimes we would have to tease him into buying the first round of drinks. All of which seemed a little odd, because he loved the limelight and continually strove to be the centre of attraction, offstage and on. I always felt that he was jealous of any other Beatle receiving more attention than he was getting.

It wasn't long before Stu became the butt of Beatle humour once more because of his association with Astrid. He would have to endure a nightly barrage of good-natured barracking or ribbing, especially when he sang his solo number, the Elvis hit *Love Me Tender*. Astrid would be sitting in the audience, her beautiful eyes gazing into his, and when he sang he was singing only to her. While he tenderly mouthed the words we would be taking the mick unmercifully with such observations as:

'He's in love again, lads!'

'He's really got it!'

'Little Cupid! Look at the wings sprouting out of his shoulders!'

'Hey! This is supposed to be a serious number – don't fall over!'

Eventually Stu would reach the point where he could take the barbs no longer. 'For Chrissake shurrup!' he would scream. And we would – for a while.

We didn't just scoff at his love-life either. He arrived at the club one night with his hair combed forward. Astrid had lent her artistic hand to achieve this effect and the result was something similar to the style that Klaus Voorman was sporting when we met him during our first trip. This was going too far, we all thought, and fell about, pointing to the fringe as though it were something that had afflicted him during the night, like a rash. His hair was swept back in the Elvis groove once more when he joined us the following evening.

However, Stu must have gone into some deep huddle with Astrid about the subject, because there he was some time later defiantly displaying the fringe again.

George soon followed suit and combed down his hair. It was another five months however, in September, before John and Paul would adopt the style, and even so it was rather short and a fair distance from their eyebrows. Personally, I kept my hair as it was, upswept, as it is to this day. No other member of the group ever made any mention to me of comforming and the style was certainly never an agreed 'must'. Nor did Brian Epstein ever give me an instruction about growing a fringe when he took over later in the year. During my time as a Beatle this style was not considered to be some sort of trademark. And who would ever have foreseen that Astrid's simple experiment with Stu would eventually result in half the male population of the world getting in on the act and some worried nations like Indonesia even going so far as to pass laws making Beatle cuts illegal!

We never had any serious rows during that second excursion to Hamburg, apart from the normal group disagreements about songs or arrangements. As always, we played long hours, and as the night wore on we might get a little shirty with each other, but this was purely confined to musical matters, like who was going to sing the next solo? Should we give the fans a rock'n'roll belter or something slower? Would we do a chorus now? All very dull on the face of it, but seemingly important on the night when tempers were likely to fray.

It was the long nightly toil that led to pill-popping – which no Beatle had indulged in on the first tour. All the stomping and clowning on stage, plus our non-stop way of life, began to take its toll. There were nights when spirits flagged and eyelids drooped and it was on one such night that Tony Sheridan held out a helping hand with the words: 'Here's something to keep you awake.' He was offering us Preludin, a type of amphetamine. It was the start of something.

I never did take advantage of the offer, even when pills were ours just for the asking. Another bottle of beer could always keep me awake; we still drank on stage at the Top Ten and the audience continued to keep us well supplied. Beer was our staple drink, but as the mood took us we might indulge in a Scotch, schnapps or maybe a vodka. 'Making show' was certainly a thirsty way to make a living. At times there were more bottles and glasses on stage than equipment, and impelled by all the exertions of 'making show,' they would frequently roll off with a thump or a crash, leaving the waiters quickly to clear up the mess.

When old friend Mutti learned that the rest of the Beatles were taking stimulants she acquired a stock from somewhere and would have them near at hand whenever we came off stage. '*Vant* some, lads?' she would ask temptingly in her fractured English. If this mysterious supply ever dried up she would only have to point a finger at one of the regulars in the audience and indicate that he or she had some.

It was a habit that I didn't deliberately try to avoid. As long as a drink pepped me up sufficiently to carry on into the small hours I never thought of using drugs. Basically it was a matter of keeping going and tubes of 'prellies' were always available.

We resumed our daily courtesy call to the Herbertstrasse and continued to fortify ourselves with bowls of cornflakes at the Seaman's Mission, so life in Hamburg resumed its normal pattern – although one thing did change. Now that we were billeted on the top floor of the premises, girls couldn't find their way up there as easily as they used to invade our Bambi Kino quarters. There were still hectic nights, but not in our dormitory.

The ladies solved the problem themselves by providing alternative accommodation and the instant orgies that were a feature of our Indra and Kaiserkeller days now ceased. In other respects little changed: we were still invited to dine and presented with little gifts – except that I narrowly escaped the vengeance of one irate husband.

Some nights Lennon and I used to take a break from routine and visit a club in the Grosse Freiheit where an Italian group were playing. An added attraction were the waitresses and there was one lovely little dolly who immediately took my eye.

I chatted her up and suggested that she come to see us at the Top Ten. She always promised that she would but stalled for some time, until one night she was in the audience. I joined her during the break and soon we became a regular twosome. All progressed smoothly until during a visit to the club where she worked, one of her colleagues took time to give me a word of warning while my girl was busy elsewhere.

'She's married, you know,' her friend told me, 'and her husband's in jail.'

'Well, I've got nothing to worry about then,' I grinned.

She didn't tell me it wouldn't be long before he came out – but I did receive another warning, this time from a second girl at the Grosse Freiheit club, who made it obvious that she fancied me. In a moment of jealousy she told me that when my girl's husband was released she was going to tell him all about my affair with his wife. 'He's one of the Hamburg hardnuts,' she said smugly.

It wasn't long after that I noticed anxiously a tough-looking man who spent the whole of one Beatles set in the Top Ten just glaring at me, never moving. Sitting behind the drums, I couldn't fail to notice him. When I left the stand after our stint and made my way to the bar for a beer, he followed me.

I felt I had to say something. 'Hello there! How you doing?' It sounded flat; the expression on his face wasn't friendly.

'You're the Beatles' drummer,' he said grimly, stating the fact rather than asking a question. I nodded. 'You know my wife,' he added; I swallowed a couple of times and had a vision of being splattered all over the Top Ten walls. 'Finish!' he growled. 'Finish!' The single word, along with the anger in his eyes, conveyed the message all right.

'Okay,' was all I said, meekly. And that seemed to be the end of it. We parted in the throng at the bar and I was relieved that I had escaped so lightly. The decent thing to do now, I decided, would be to amble round to the Grosse Freiheit and tell his wife that we were through.

At the entrance of her club, the doorman seemed agitated. 'Don't come in, Pete,' he pleaded, 'the girl's husband is after you!'

'I must see her,' I said, brushing the warning aside, as I had already met the husband. 'It'll only take five minutes.'

'Let me pass the message on,' the doorman volunteered, but I slipped in past him and found the waitress. There was fear in her eyes when she saw me.

'My husband's going to beat the hell out of you!' she said, almost in tears.

Then the doorman rushed to tell me that her husband had been sighted, having trailed me from the Top Ten. 'Get into the gents and lock yourself in!' the doorman said. 'I'll let you know when it's safe to come out.'

I dashed into a cubicle, sat on the toilet and put my feet up against the door so that the man shouldn't see them if he came looking. I waited there for about half an hour, trying not to make a sound while he rampaged around in search for me. I was still in one piece when he gave up and departed.

Then I had a few words with his wife, telling her that this had to be the end of the affair. She agreed that we should never meet again. As I left, the doorman was nursing a black eye received when he tried to bar the husband's path, but he recovered enough to warn me once more: 'If ever this guy sees you around here he's going to snuff you out!' And I didn't doubt it.

But this wasn't the end, because in spite of her husband, the girl came to the Top Ten to see me a couple of times after that eventful night. Two weeks after the episode, her husband turned up too; I spotted him from the stage and even from there could see that he was drunk and in the mood for trouble. Suddenly he spurted into action, heading in my direction, eyes blazing. He thumped waiters aside, clambered over tables, sending drinks flying, and succeeded in climbing unsteadily on to the stage.

The Beatles were in the middle of a number. I reached down and gripped one of the beer bottles that always littered the stand, at the same time still trying to keep the rhythm going. The rest of the group started to whistle for some inexplicable reason while he closed in on me and thrust a husky arm towards my neck. I was just about to lift the bottle to crash over his head when he collapsed onto me, so drunk he didn't even have the strength to get his fingers round my throat or aim a punch. He began to slobber over me, incapable. Thankfully we reached the end of the number and I was able to disentangle myself. I hauled the man to his feet and we staggered together to the bar, where there was only one thing left to do: buy each other a drink. After that I never saw him again ... or his wife.

Life was seldom dull along the Reeperbahn; on one memorable occasion on this second tour the Beatles even found themselves providing the background music to a battle between the Canadian Army and the staff of the Top Ten.

The Canadian Army – not quite all of it, but a sizeable chunk, running into hundreds – came to town on leave and took over the whole of the Reeperbahn, scores of them making a frontal assault on the club while we were in session. It was like the Dieppe raid all over again in its ferocity. The Top Ten was already crowded when the invasion began and it was typical of servicemen on the loose. We had seen it all before but not in such numbers: they would down the drinks – then refuse to pay up when the bill arrived.

Usually the waiters would be able to cope using their deadly little truncheons or, if need be, the deadlier gas gun. Pay up or be beaten up was a choice that most often ended with the serviceman reaching for his wallet. But this time it was different. Fists began to fly in every corner of the club and the waiters and bouncers were outnumbered. Peter Eckhorn, cool in command, sent for reinforcements – not the cops but more waiters, who were like an army in their own right, backed up by a collection of the Hamburg hard-nuts with which St Pauli abounded.

The manoeuvre paid off and the Canadian trouble-makers were tossed out on their ears – but unfortunately Peter Eckhorn wasn't the only one who could call on reinforcements. The defeated Canucks hurriedly rustled up a few hundred more of their compatriots and within a short time marched on the Top Ten, bent on retribution.

A long passage led off the Reeperbahn into the club and, as word of the impending counter-attack seeped through, it was here that Eckhorn decided to make his stand behind a barricade hastily erected by his henchmen, while the Beatles continued to pound out rock'n'roll and people continued to dance. Tables were piled high in the passage and behind them Eckhorn's fusiliers waited to go into action. Tony Sheridan was trying to sing with us as battle was joined to the accompaniment of whoops and shouts and the noise of crashing furniture and splintering glass.

'Good God!' Tony cried, breaking off, 'the place is going to be wrecked!'

We manfully soldiered on as waiters, toughies and soldiers pitched into each other in a 1961 re-run of World World II. The din was now doing its best to drown us and the paying customers who had come to listen or dance began to find the battle more interesting than the talents of Sheridan, Lennon, McCartney and the rest of the Beatles.

Nothing was safe any more. The Canadians tore the glass-fronted showcases from the passage walls, where our pictures were displayed. Bottles were being hurled like hand-grenades in every direction and tables clawed from the barricade were hurtling into the defenders.

'They're bloody mad!' Paul yelled when the Canadians managed somehow to start a fire at the makeshift barrier.

Like a general waiting to see the whites of their eyes, Eckhorn decided to play his ace and bring his artillery into action. About twenty waiters were given the order to fire their gas guns as the mass of Canadians were about to burst through the barricade. Fumes filled the passage and the entrance to the main club room, the clouds spilling back inside until even our eyes began to smart. But it meant victory for Eckhorn. The battle simmered down amid a chorus of shouts and screams as the gas performed its deadly task, knocking the fight out of the visitors, who began to retreat to the fresh air on the Reeperbahn, dragging their wounded by the feet. Incredibly, the fighting, growing uglier by the minute, had gone on for almost two hours, and the police only arrived as it died down, arresting about 30 Canadians as they fled.

What was left of the night passed off quickly after the smoke had lifted and the debris had been cleared. But Peter Eckhorn was taking no chances. 'I'm sure they won't take this lying down,' he said. 'We'll be ready for them if they return.'

In the event only two returned – the following night. They were sober and mannerly. 'We've come back to apologize,' they said meekly.

Around this time the Beatles injected a new style of entertainment to the Reeperbahn. For the sheer hell of it we would start at the top of the street and work our way to the bottom of it – playing leap-frog. We would keep going until we almost collapsed, not even bothering to stop when a traffic light showed red. Sometimes we wouldn't be able to muster enough strength to clear each other's backs and would sprawl in a heap. We became a familiar sight and members of the public would join in, a long trail of Germans of varying ages all leap-frogging behind us: it was complete madness. At some intersections friendly cops would hold up the traffic to wave us through. Try to imagine it happening in London's Oxford Street on a busy shopping day and you will get some idea of the lunacy. But this was the kind of crazy behaviour the Germans had learned to expect of the Beatles.

Our clothing suffered as a result. On a dull day with damp coming in off the sea we would collect Hamburg's dirt and dust as we rolled exhausted in the gutters of the Reeperbahn. Jeans would get torn and there would have to be the usual sewing job.

One afternoon, as a change of routine, we dared Paul to don a pith helmet we had acquired somewhere and march up and down the Reeperbahn like a German sentry with a broom for a rifle. He rolled up his jeans about six inches – they were too tight to get them to his knees

– and entered into the challenge, covering the twenty yards or so to the end of the block, then turning. Encouraged by the rest of us, he broke into a smart goose-step while we screamed '*Sieg Heil*!' at him. Hamburg citizens passing by simply glanced at Paul or shrugged. If they were offended they never showed it.

For his reward we let Paul keep the helmet and celebrated his escapade by filling it with beer – which ran out through the sweatholes; that didn't please him all that much.

Some of the steam went out of our merry-go-round way of life when Cynthia and Paul's girlfriend Dot, a blonde shop assistant he met during the old Casbah days, arrived for a stay of a few weeks during Cyn's Easter vacation from college.

Cyn was befriended by Astrid and spent some of her nights as a guest of the Kirchherr family. Old friend Mutti offered to accommodate Dot on a convenient houseboat she owned and where Cyn sometimes joined her. But there were nights when the two girls trooped upstairs to our dormitory, and on these occasions George and I would be instructed not to claim our bunks until four o'clock in the morning. If the holiday-makers, weary of sight-seeing, came into our quarters during the afternoon, George and I would be requested tactfully to 'look the other way'.

There was little to occupy Cyn and Dot once they had done the sights and visited the shops in the more respectable area of the city, guided by Astrid, who drove them around in her grey VW Beetle. In the evening the girls had a choice of either sitting around in the Top Ten and watching us 'making show' with Tony Sheridan for seven or eight hours, or wandering off to the dormitory to escape the ear-splitting noise. When they did choose to take refuge upstairs, John and Paul would drift off during a session a visit them, then rejoin us on stage later.

The German fans couldn't fail to notice that two of their favourite idols had imported a couple of rivals from England. Some of them, especially those whose beds we sometimes shared, would sit and glare, treating the Beatles to an angry silence when it was time to applaud.

One night some German lads, discovering that Cyn and Dot were English visitors but without knowing the background, started to chat them up at a Top Ten table. It all seemed innocent enough at the outset, but the British girls made it obvious that they were not the least interested in the attention now being paid to them. The German boys persisted and reached the pawing stage. Paul, who frequently doubled on piano during this second tour, couldn't really see what was going on, but Lennon and I could. Right from the start in the Casbah, John was always very jealous whenever Cyn was around; if anyone tried to talk to her while he was playing Lennon would try to wither them with a laser-like glare. Once off-stage they would be abruptly told to 'fuck off'.

It was plain that night in the Top Ten that the two girls were now a little scared. At the end of the number, the heavy mob of Lennon and Best hurried down from the dais and sailed in to save them. In his usual blunt manner, John handed out a verbal lashing and for a few moments a nasty scene threatened to develop.

'Why are you butting in?' one of the Germans asked arrogantly, sparring for trouble, which resulted in some pushing and jostling.

'That's my girlfriend you're messing about with,' John snarled at him.

The situation immediately began to cool, and the apologies followed. The Germans explained that they thought the girls were simply British tourists looking for fun; what's more, they went on, they themselves were Beatle fans and would never think of trying to upset us.

After this near-miss the waiters, ever dutiful, made a point of hovering near Cyn and Dot like watchful guard dogs. There was never any more trouble after that one incident. And when the girls left for home our faithful German ravers (the female ones, that is) called off their silent protest and were all smiles again.

Strangely, we never saw Bruno Koschmieder again; during our brief sojourn in Liverpool his star seemed to have faded. Not long after our arrival we gingerly crept round to take a peep at the Kaiserkeller, to find it looking something like a ghost-town saloon. Nothing was going on, except for a few people playing the pin-tables on the way in. You could see down into the club from street level and we noticed that the number of slot machines had been increased since our departure. In the cut-throat war for the favours of St Pauli, Peter Eckhorn had won one more battle.

Astrid Kirchherr and Stu Sutcliffe.

A collector's item – the Beatles' first single, produced in Hamburg by Bert Kaempfert.

8

JOHN, PAUL, GEORGE AND PETE

By mid-May Stuart Sutcliffe could stand the taunts no longer; breaking point came one night at the Top Ten while we were backing Tony Sheridan. Paul was at the piano as usual for Tony's act when he said something about Astrid that must have really hurt. Stu had been used to the harmless ribbing which frayed his temper occasionally; it usually stopped when he protested strongly, but whatever Paul said that night – I never did find out – really struck home.

Although normally something of a pacifist, this time Stu dropped his bass guitar, stormed across the stage to the piano and landed Paul such a wallop that it knocked him off his stool. Meanwhile Tony was continuing his song at the mike. Paul and Stu began struggling on the floor of the stand, rolling round locked in the most ferocious battle. Tony began to dry up, but then recovered and started to shout his lyrics.

Paul and Stu fought on, a fury of flailing fists, exchanging punch for punch for around five minutes – until the number ended and we prised them apart to applause from the audience. They were accustomed to John and Paul's mock battles in the cause of 'making show', but I doubt if any of them could have fooled themselves into believing that this was all part of the act.

When battle had ceased, Stu raged at Paul: 'Don't you ever say anything about Astrid again, or I'll beat the brains out of you!'

'I'll say what I like!' Paul yelled back.

They argued on and off for the rest of the night; it was the beginning of the end of Stu as a Beatle: the crunch had arrived. I suppose he had just had enough of the wisecracks about his love affair, about the way Astrid had transformed him even to his hairstyle; and about his poor showing on guitar – most of the criticism in this area coming from Paul and John. Anyway Stu had, in fact, reached the stage where he no longer needed the Beatles or the nightly slanging matches and had been considering quitting for some time. His relationship with Astrid was completely fulfilling and marriage would follow at some time. That she was three years older than him presented no problem; they were soulmates, both artistic. It was his deep devotion to art that was pulling at him as well; he planned to further his studies in Hamburg and forsake the aimless twanging of bass guitar while a bunch of clowns cavorted around a stage.

Nevertheless, his friendship with us all continued after the big fight with Paul and the break, when it came, was clean and friendly and completely devoid of recrimination. It coincided with the next development along the road to fame: the entry into our lives of Bert Kaempfert, and the cutting of our first record.

Bert was already a name known around the world. He led a big sweet-music German orchestra and penned melodic songs of his own, of which the best known would be the classic *Strangers In The Night*, a world hit for Frank Sinatra. Kaempfert was in his early thirties when he began to drift into the Top Ten. It was hardly his scene, this middle-of-the-road music man who chalked up orchestral successes in Britain and the United States with such standards as *Bye Bye Blues* and *Three O'clock In The Morning* – a long way from the belting Mersey beat that blasted the Top Ten till the small hours.

Bert was, however, searching for talent in his other role as a record producer for the German Polydor label, but he found what he was looking for in Tony Sheridan rather than the Beatles. We never saw Bert during his sorties into the club and only knew that he had been present when Peter Eckhorn told us. He certainly showed little excitement at what we were doing, remarking some years later: 'It is obvious that they were enormously talented, but nobody – including the boys themselves – knew how to use it or where that talent would lead them.'

However, we were a natural choice to back Tony when Bert decided to launch him as a solo singer on Polydor. Tony had made it plain that he would feel more at home if we were in the studio with him, and Bert had anyway been impressed by an instrumental we had been playing regularly at the Top Ten – a piece called *Cry For A Shadow*, which had a dubious origin but was well received by the crowd.

Cry For A Shadow had been born during our first Hamburg tour, the result of trying to take the mickey out of Rory Storm. It had virtually been put together by George Harrison in a few minutes after Rory had called in on us during a rehearsal at the Kaiserkeller. He was telling us how much he liked the Shadows' song *Frightened City*. 'Can you play it?' he asked. 'It goes like this,' he added, starting to sing the opening bars.

George intentionally began to play around the Shadows' melody in a sort of counterpart – without Rory having the slightest suspicion that he was being sent up. Lennon joined in and I picked up the beat. What emerged was a catchy little number in unmistakable Shadows' style which we liked well enough to include in our repertoire. Even the title we gave it later – *Cry For A Shadow* – was something of a pun.

In a way, I suppose, this was something of a tribute to George and his undeniable song-writing talent. Music always came first with him, ahead of birds and booze. During those long, tiring hours of 'making show', George kept at his task seriously, always preoccupied with the kind of noise he was producing and whether or not it was coming out right.

He was always trying to improve the sound. In Hamburg he bought a new Gibson amplifier that was not available in Britain at that time; in Liverpool, between tours, he bought an American Gretsch guitar (a move Lennon copied). One more cherished addition of George's was a twang-arm or vibrator. There was never any suggestion that the rest of us should share these expenses, either. George would always use his own money ultimately for the benefit of us all.

Now the great Bert Kaempfert had awakened to George's composing talent, despite its background of mickey-taking. Bert used to request the number during those Top Ten visits, along with *My Bonnie* and *The Saints* – two of Tony Sheridan's offerings, based on the popular standards *My Bonnie Lies Over The Ocean* and *When The Saints Go Marching In* – and *Ain't She Sweet*, a standard that Lennon used to sing.

Naturally we were pretty excited when we found out that we were going to cut our first disc around the end of May – even though the session promised little more than a back seat, with Tony Sheridan up front as the star. But we all felt it was another step forward, and once in the studio – who could tell? – we might be able to bend Bert's ear with some of the material we preferred, including a few originals.

Shortly before our recording date with Bert, another epic fight occurred between myself and our old friend Tony Sheridan. Tony had been pestering me to play some particular arrangement of his on drums, but I insisted that I preferred to do things my way. He droned on and on about it, ending up by snapping. 'Do it the way I want it next time!'

'Get knotted!' I told him.

This made him mad. 'Okay!' he flared, 'there's only one way to settle this – I'll see you outside!'

This is the way Tony himself described the event in a *New Musical Express* interview in 1964, and I can't quarrel with his version:

'Our day began at about two in the afternoon, when we would swagger down to the Seaman's Mission for a meal ... Then we'd meet our friends and go down to the club and do the stint. Sometimes it would last six hours or more. What a jumping place that was. Go, go, go, there all the time.

'One day, however, things did actually stop. Pete Best and I had been arguing music policy for some time and it had come to a head that night. We stopped playing right in the middle of a number and got ready for a punch-up.

'The audience were yelling and goading us on. But we didn't scrap until after the club was closed.

'Down a dark alley we had the physical argument. The fight lasted about two hours and at the end of it Pete and I were the best of friends. Have been ever since. I've still got the marks of that bust-up though.'

At which point in the interview Tony showed the reporter his knuckles. 'They were blotched red and lined,' the writer revealed – three years after the slogging match!

A more immediate problem, however, had been Stu. It had already been decided among the rest of us that he would not take part in the recording session because, it was agreed, the more experienced Paul would make a better showing on bass guitar. I believe Stu had guessed that this might happen, and the embarrassment of having to tell him never arose. Instead he broke the news to us that he wanted to leave the Beatles to concentrate on his art studies and planned to stay on in Hamburg for this purpose when our Top Ten residency expired.

'It's up to you, Stu,' was the reply from the remaining Beatles. 'No one wants you to leave, you know that.' But he was already determined and brushed aside all the niceties that you find yourself mouthing at times such as this. His exit was all cut and dried in one night. No dithering, no soul-searching, no postponing and no bitterness. 'I've been thinking of leaving for a long time,' he explained, and that was final. But he continued to come and see us with Astrid almost every night.

When the great day of our debut arrived, four bleary-eyed Beatles left for the Polydor studio around 8am after only four hours in bed. We must have looked something like sleep-walkers when we reached it.

Studio? We wondered if we had come to the right place. We had been expecting a recording set-up on the grand scale; after all Bert was a big name and Polydor an important label, part of the Deutsche Grammophon company. Instead we found ourselves in an unexciting school hall with a massive stage and lots of drapes. The recording equipment was backstage; we were expected to play behind Tony on the stage – as if the whole thing was an outside broadcast. Surely this couldn't be the place where Bert made his own smoochy bestsellers? It was – and he was perfectly satisfied with the conditions.

And so to work. Fortified with bottles of Coke to help keep us awake, we ploughed into several takes of *My Bonnie*, experimenting with different intros. All appeared to be going well until George Harrison knocked over a Coke bottle, producing a crash that sounded like a thunderclap on the tape.

'All Coke bottles off the stage!' Bert yelled. 'That could have been a very good take!' He appeared to be angry, but he was, we found, a very nice guy.

Backing Tony, we also recorded *The Saints* along with a song of his own called *Why* and one more traditional number, *If You Love Me Baby (Take Out Some Insurance On Me, Baby)*. The Beatles were given a chance to show what they could do when Kaempfert agreed to hear us out with a batch of Lennon and McCartney songs; they failed signally to make him jump up and down with excitement. As far as Bert was concerned, the world was not yet ready for the Beatles doing their own thing. He settled instead for John singing *Ain't She Sweet* and George's suspect *Cry For A Shadow*.

Bert played it safe by releasing first *My Bonnie* and *The Saints*. They were arranged by Tony Sheridan himself. On the label we were called the Beat Brothers because Bert thought the word 'Beatles' was confusing for Germans. The fact that some wags called us the Peedles might also have had some bearing on his decision, *peedle* being a slang word for the male appendage. *My Bonnie* and *The Saints* did reasonably well in Germany – while our two sides without Tony collected a layer of dust on the Polydor shelves. They wouldn't be unleashed on the world at large until the Beatles had finally crashed the barriers to international fame.

Even if Tony Sheridan had sold a million copies of *My Bonnie* when it was first released it wouldn't have put any extra marks into our pockets. We were simply used as session men on the record and each received a flat fee of £20 with no royalty clause attached. We spent the money getting drunk that same night. But it would be *My Bonnie* that would lead Brian Epstein to seek out the Beatles before the year was through. He would also have to seek out Bert Kaempfert at some stage because we had signed a year's contract with Bert. (We did another session with Tony for him, recording *Sweet Georgia Brown* and *Skinny Minny*.) But whatever the details of the contract – I don't recall them at all – Kaempfert waived them all for Epstein. Asked years later if he had any regrets, he answered that he had none and went on: 'People say to me, "You must be very sad today, you would be a millionaire." I always smile and say "What would I do with a second million, anyway?" But seriously, I make my money from records. I am happy.' (Bert Kaempfert died suddenly on holiday in Majorca in the summer of 1980 after completing a British tour. He was 57.)

Our second trip to Hamburg really was very pleasant apart from the few scraps. Even the departure of Stu had not been too painful. We were no longer desperately short of cash either. We never did roll in it, but we were able to smarten up somewhat, and apart from buying the leather trousers, we later splashed out on brown suede overcoats. When the time arrived for us to catch the boat train home to Liverpool, leaving Hamburg proved to be a terrific wrench, in marked contrast to our rag-tag exit of the previous winter. Never had the Beatles displayed so much collective sentiment. We all wept, real salt tears.

We downed a few farewell beers before starting to pack in the dormitory. Horst Fascher, the tough Koschmieder defector, was there feeling as long-faced as we did. We reminisced about the good times as we stuffed our gear into suitcases. Horst began to cry; we were fighting back the tears, but not for long – soon they were streaming down our cheeks, and the dormitory that had been the scene of so many laughs were now full of sniffles and snuffles.

'Come on, lads!' George Harrison said, 'let's not be stupid.'

Downstairs it was worse. A dozen or so weeping girl fans were waiting for us along with a bunch of sad-eyed waiters. Veterans of the great battle with the Canadian Army put their strong arms round our shoulders in a fond adieu which fetched more tears to all our eyes.

Between sobs and sighs the girls pleaded 'Write to us. Don't forget! We love you!'

The Germans, I had found, were seldom over-emotional. Nor for that matter were the Beatles, but everyone felt that this was like a family parting; all the kissing, the embracing, the handshakes. We sought solace in a few more bottles of beer and found it was even more difficult to stem the flood of tears.

Well-wishers started running to keep pace with the taxi when we began the ten-minute journey to the railway station. Those that waited outside the Top Ten entrance waved until the cab was out of sight. John, Paul, George and I sat in silence, staring into space.

Stu and Astrid were at the station to see us off; they bought us some food and Cokes and lemonade. Then the tears began to well up again. Stu was staying on, of course, happy that he would be devoting his energies to art and that Astrid would be at his side to support him. There would be a long gap before the Beatles returned to headline the opening of the swish new Star Club in the Grosse Freheit, and there would be more tears – of a different kind – when we next set foot on German soil.

9

CAVERN CAPERS

Back at the Cavern in July 1961 we sweated it out even more in our black leather pants. The Liverpool dandruff continued to drip from the ceilings, the fans swelled in number and carried on fainting in the warmer climate of summer. Now that we were recording stars (or so we thought) and I was still acting as manager of the Beatles, I did what a manager was supposed to do – I upped the fee for our performances. No more £5 and £6 sessions. We were on our way and we could now demand £20 a time. Naturally there were promoters who bleated that they wouldn't book us any more at this inflated price, but we were no longer prepared to play for peanuts.

Mo was the first to pay up – there were going to be no on-the-cheap performances at the Casbah either. She was businesslike herself and readily understood that there was no room for family favours. She paid us £18 instead of the earlier £5, a raise of more than 200 per cent.

The Cavern came up trumps as well and three lunchtime sessions a week brought us £30 – double our earlier fee. With evening bookings at £20 a time and other engagements, we were sharing well over £100 a week. But there was no rest; we still played six days a week, sometimes seven. 'Let's get the cash in!' was the motto. When the protesting promoters realized how many customers we could now draw there was no more holding back and we were paid the sum we asked. These financial arrangements were left completely in my hands. Not one of the other Beatles ever suggested that perhaps I was setting our sights too high or over-pricing the group. We never discussed or argued about this side of the business and I simply tackled it on my own.

On our return from Hamburg we shed our title for one night only and joined forces with Gerry and the Pacemakers for a knockabout appearance as the Beatmakers, a Brian Kelly promotion at Litherland Town Hall. There was the usual clowning and romping around, plus swapping of instruments and some odd solos delivered on paper and comb. Lennon was featured on piano and there were two drummers,

Freddie Marsden (Gerry's brother) and myself.

Inspired by the remarkable Astrid, John and Paul had returned from Germany with two new items in their baggage – cameras, which they had bought there. Their original intention may have been to try and capture in Liverpool some of the vividly contrasting studies in light and shade in which the artistic Astrid had specialized, but it didn't exactly work out like that. At the Cavern they set themselves up as glamour cameramen – with distinctly sexual overtones.

John started the ball rolling, or rather the shutter clicking. He would single out a fan at one of our lunchtime sessions, chat her up and proposition her about posing for some pictures. Afterwards he would regale us with the intimate details. 'Got her with her briefs on!' he would chuckle. 'Couldn't get her bra off – but coooooo!'

After this Paul decided to jump on the bandwagon. After the Cavern appearances out would come the cameras from their leather jackets and then the search for talent would begin. The pair of them were not yet advanced enough in photography to develop or print themselves so the films would go to a chemist – who frequently blacked out the more meaty poses and sent back only the decent ones. Those that escaped censorship usually showed girls straddling chairs, girls showing a leg or two, girls with a leg in the air, girls minus some of their clothing. One girl named Pat became so hooked that she went into business as a model, taking it all really seriously, which John and Paul certainly didn't.

Although George and I didn't take up the hobby we had the same sexual appetites and enjoyed the results of their endeavours which we all crowded round to see. John, who didn't mind describing himself as 'a great wanker from way back' was highly delighted with some of his efforts. 'I've had a great session,' he would tell us, 'I pulled a couple of birds – but not a word to Cyn!'

Cynthia would often arrive at Mathew Street for our evening appearances – and so perhaps would a girl who had been posing for John in the afternoon. When the girl beamed a knowing smile his way he would switch off, as if he had never seen her before in his life or, if near enough, give a quick innocuous 'Hello', for fear of Cynthia stumbling on to his secret.

To us he would enthuse about the poses, with descriptive phrases such as: 'When we started off she just sat on the stool. Then I got her to show a bit more leg, then a bit more. And then she took her sweater off. Fantastic afternoon – I'm buggered!'

'But you've only been taking photographs!' George or I would comment, mock-innocently.

A chemist who handed back only a few prints would be quickly upbraided with: 'Where's the rest of the reel?'

'Sir,' he would be told, 'we do not print this kind of pornography.'

Previous page: Before and after! Main picture: Backstage at the Cavern, featuring black leather and swept-back hair. Inset: George and Paul on stage – now the so-called 'Beatle cut' has been born.

* THE CAVERN PRESENTS

A RIVERBOAT SHUFFLE

FRIDAY, 25TH AUG. 1961.

ABOARD THE

" M.V. ROYAL IRIS "

WITH

MR. ACKER BILK'S

PARAMOUNT JAZZ BAND

And THE BEATLES

BOAT SAILS AT 7.45 P.M.
FROM LIVERPOOL LANDING STAGE
RETURNING AT 11.0 P.M.

Tickets 8/6

Telephone
Hoylake 1136.

Brookside,
Heron Road,
Meols,
Ches.

19th. August, 1961

Mr. P. Best, Mr.
8, Hymans Green,
Liverpool 12.

Dear Mr. Best,

Will you let me have your terms for the services of the Beetles to pay at Hoylake Y.M.C.A. from 8-0 p.m. till 11-0 p.m., and if you are available on Friday, the 8th. Sept. next.

As I am going away from home in two days time, I would appreciate it if you could let me have this information by return. You can get me on the phone at the above no. on Monday or Tuesday mornings.

We have other dates, but this is the present urgent one as I wish to fix it before going away.

Yours faithfully,

Chas. K. Tranter

Chas. K. Tranter.

'What about the negatives?' John wanted to know.

'We've confiscated them.'

'Bloody prude,' was how John dismissed him.

He was convinced that these offending chemists were perverts at heart who spent most of their time 'out back wanking themselves off' over his labours in the cause of art.

'And what do I get out of it?' John would lament. 'Just a bunch of these rotten stills!'

George and I would rib him: 'But it's the other ones *we* want to see – not these.'

'So do I,' he would grunt. 'Sod off!'

We also used to send up some of the girls who posed for these budding David Baileys.

'Had your photographs taken then, have you?' we would wink.

'How'd you know?'

'Been looking at a couple of snaps. Still wearing black drawers?'

It was all in good humour and the girls knew damn well that the 'art studies' of them weren't going to be kept under lock and key somewhere. These glamour sessions were usually held in accommodation provided by the girls. I doubt if Paul's Dad would have stood for it at his home, or John's Aunt Mimi at hers.

Lennon's off-beat sense of humour was now being put before the public in increasing volume, both in front of audiences and in print. It would be there at the Cavern when he announced the next number in our programme. 'This is a record by Chuck Berry,' he would say, deadpan, 'a Liverpool-born white singer with bandy legs and no hair!' Some uninitiated members would nod knowingly, believing this nutty description of the great Negro cult figure – while the rest of us would be near collapse at their gullibility.

Sometimes the club's cleaners would be around and call for requests. 'Here's one for Aggie,' John would say, 'who's got her foot stuck in a bucket!'

He hated having to make a straightforward announcement. He would juggle the names of artists around. 'Chuck Vincent' and 'Gene Berry' were two favourites, always delivered with a serious face, but he rarely used the same patter twice.

One day he announced that Bob Wooler was his father, whom he hadn't seen for fifteen years. Some of the customers actually believed him and Wooler, to his credit, played along for a while, agreeing when tackled that this was indeed true. Few people knew that John hadn't actually seen his real father, the sea-faring Freddie Lennon, for that same amount of years. Freddie would arrive back on the scene only after John had found the fame he had long yearned for.

Wooler suffered several Beatles' tricks in those days. He would have

Town Hall

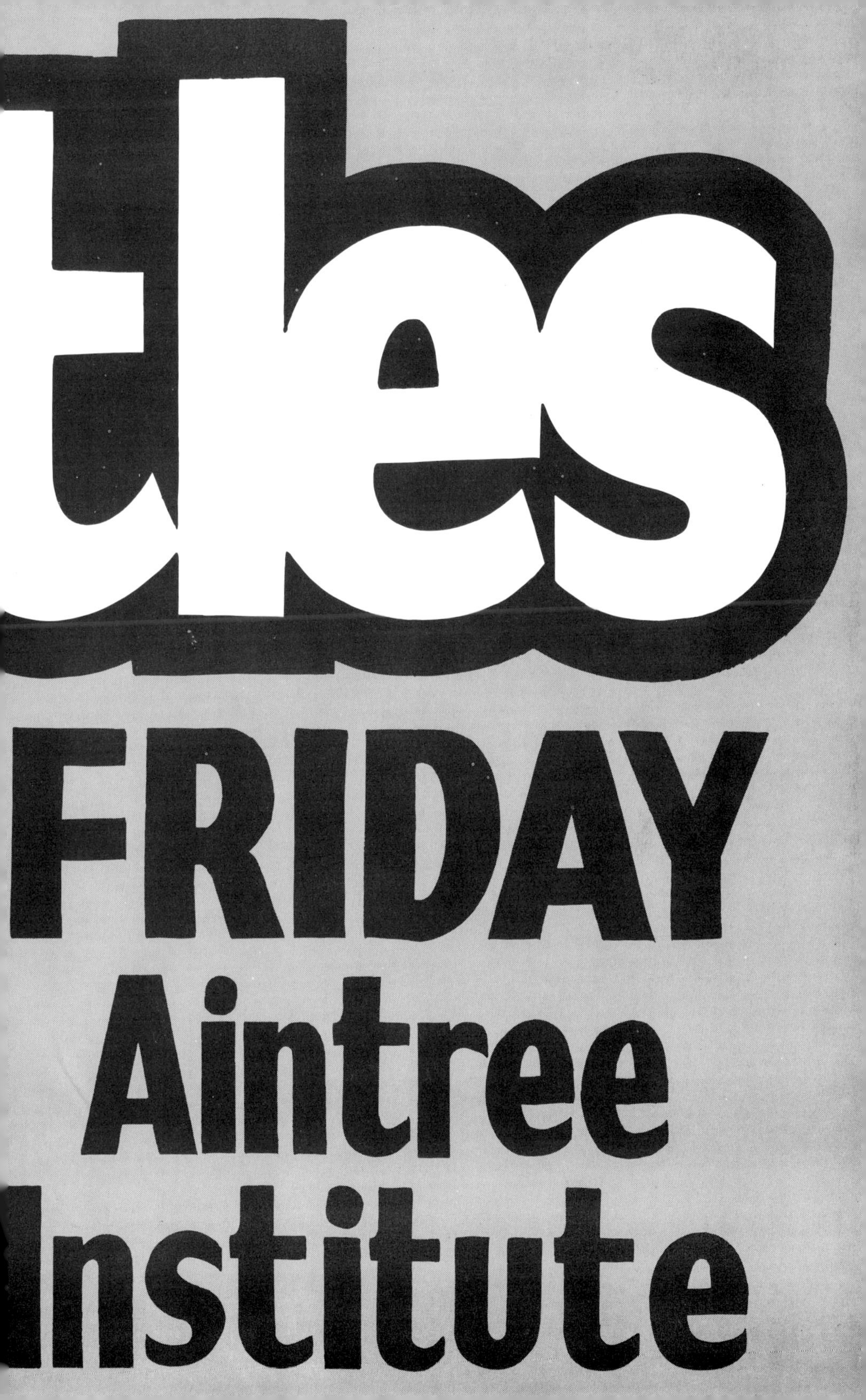
tles
FRIDAY
Aintree
nstitute

carefully sorted his records for his Cavern DJ show, stacking them in order ready to slot in with his chat without having to study the label when the time came. While he was looking the other way one of us would mix them up or substitute entirely different discs. He took it in good part, and managed to get his own back from time to time. He usually introduced us with a recording of a fanfare, but there were days when he presented the 'fabulous Beatles' to the strains of Ruby Murray singing *Softly, Softly* or some such offering far removed from a fanfare of trumpets or the big beat.

In spare moments Lennon was always scribbling on odd pieces of paper or envelopes, writing strange little stories with crazy mixed-up phrases, or scrawling his mis-shapen figures with long noses and drooping bellies from one side of the paper to the other. During that July of 1961 his old pal Bill Harry launched the *Mersey Beat* pop paper and featured on the first front page a 'short diversion on the dubious origins of the Beatles, translated from the John Lennon'.

Bill had invited him to make this contribution, which he received on the usual scraps of paper. In the issue dated July 6–20, part of it lightheartedly records my recruitment to the group and the disasters of that first Hamburg tour.

John wrote that 'a man with a beard cut off said – will you go to Germany (Hamburg) and play mighty rock for the peasants for money? And we said we would play mighty anything for money.

'But before we could go we had to grow a drummer, so we grew one in West Derby in a club called Some Casbah and his trouble was Pete Best. We called "Hello Pete, come off to Germany!" "Yes!" Zooooom. After a few months, Peter and Paul (who is called McArtrey, son of Jim McArtrey, his father) lit a Kino (cinema) and the German police said "Bad Beatles, you must go home and light your English cinemas". Zooooom, half a group...'

In the van on the way to a gig Lennon would lose himself in one of his fantasies, scribbling and sketching. One night, I recall, he was exploring beneath the waves and seeing in his mind all kinds of crazy marine life, such as the 'eightcat' (octopus) and 'squint' (squid), apart from swimming fish cakes. He was caught up, he explained, 'by the "ruptures" of the deep.' In the not far distant future these and other doodlings would be published in book form and take their place in the nation's bestseller lists.

On stage he would often try to get laughs at the expense of Paul, whose favourite oldie ballad at this time was still *Over The Rainbow* (later it would be *Till There Was You*).

Paul, blinking his big brown eyes at the girls in the audience, would announce that he had received lots of requests for *Over The Rainbow*, at which John would prop himself against the Cavern piano and burst into

Clowning at a photo-session. Pete (foreground) is about to go under; but George and Paul are 'head and shoulders' above the rest.

"OPERATION BIG BEAT II"

in the Tower Ballroom, New Brighton

on Friday, 24th November 1961

7-30 p.m. to 2-00 a.m.

More Rocking to Merseysides Top Six Groups:-

THE BEATLES - - RORY STORM AND THE HURRICANES
GERRY AND THE PACEMAKERS - FARON AND THE FLAMINGOES
THE REMO FOUR - EARL PRESTON AND THE TEMPEST TORNADOES

Three Licensed Bars (until 12-45 a.m.) *Buffet*

LATE TRANSPORT (Liverpool, Wirral and Cheshire)

Excursions Leaving St. John's Lane (Lime Street) 7-00 p.m. to 9-00 p.m.

TICKET 6/-

raucous laugh, followed by: 'God! He's doing Judy Garland!' while Paul's fans whispered, nudged each other expectantly and simmered with 'ooohs' and 'aaahs'.

John would play seriously for a while as Paul gave his emotional all to the song; then John would suddenly start to pull a grotesque face or adopt his wicked hunchback pose against the piano, head tucked into his shoulders, features contorted. Eyes in the audience would begin to stray from Paul and some laughter would follow, gathering pace at John's antics. Paul would get mad and on occasion have to stop in the middle of his ballad. Then he and John would both start clowning. Another of John's tricks during these solo offerings of Paul's was to produce a series of weird sounds from his guitar that intruded into the melody like sore thumbs. Again Paul would not be too pleased and John would gaze around the stage in all innocence.

Such was the interest being shown in us now that a fan club emerged, formed by some of the girls at the Cavern, an impromptu and well-meaning demonstration of affection but executed with little knowhow. It was our first fan club, however, and we were grateful for it, especially when the members collected £5 between them to stage the inaugural club night in a room upstairs in the David Lewis Theatre, a fine old building which had seen better days, situated near Liverpool's Anglican Cathedral.

We were scheduled to give a performance for no fee, which might have hurt a little but not all that much, seeing that we were the objects of so much devotion. Sadly, it was not much of a night to remember. We had expected to find a huge crowd gathered there, but only some sixty people turned up. We had no PA system with us, a couple of amps had fused and we spent most of the time sitting on the edge of the stage chatting to the birds under the watchful eye of Paul's father.

There were requests for favourite Beatles' numbers, which were delivered without any aid of a mike. I was asked to sing *Matchbox* and *Peppermint Twist*, a couple of my solos that were featured at the Cavern, and a Presley number, *A Rose Grows Wild In The Country*. I couldn't remember all the lyrics of that one, so when I dried up I went into a semi-Presley act, leaping around, then leaning down and greeting the fans with a handshake, wound up like some clockwork doll.

Paul's father was delighted. 'You've broken the atmosphere,' he said, 'it was dying a death.'

Paul did his best as well, singing his ballads, but generally it was a dismal night of complete failure, having suffered from lack of publicity. Before I left the group, an official fan club was finally formed and these gatherings were held at the Cavern itself. There they were an immense success, with so many people crowding in that they were bouncing off the ceiling.

Paramount Enterprises

DANCE AND CONCERT PROMOTION ETC.

TELEPHONE NEW BRIGHTON 1232

PARTNERS:
L.W. DODD D.E.H. DODD

67 SEABANK ROAD
WALLASEY CHESHIRE

LWD/VJ

25th August, 1961.

Mr. Peter Best,
8, Haymans Green,
WEST DERBY,
Liverpool.

Dear Sir,

"THE BEATLES"

I have pleasure in enclosing Contract covering an engagement of the above group at the Grosvenor Ballroom, Wallasey, on Friday, 15th September, at the agreed fee of £15. 0. 0. all in.

Will you please sign the original Contract and this must be returned immediately, the pink copy to be retained for your files.

Yours faithfully,
PARAMOUNT ENTERPRISES

Encls.

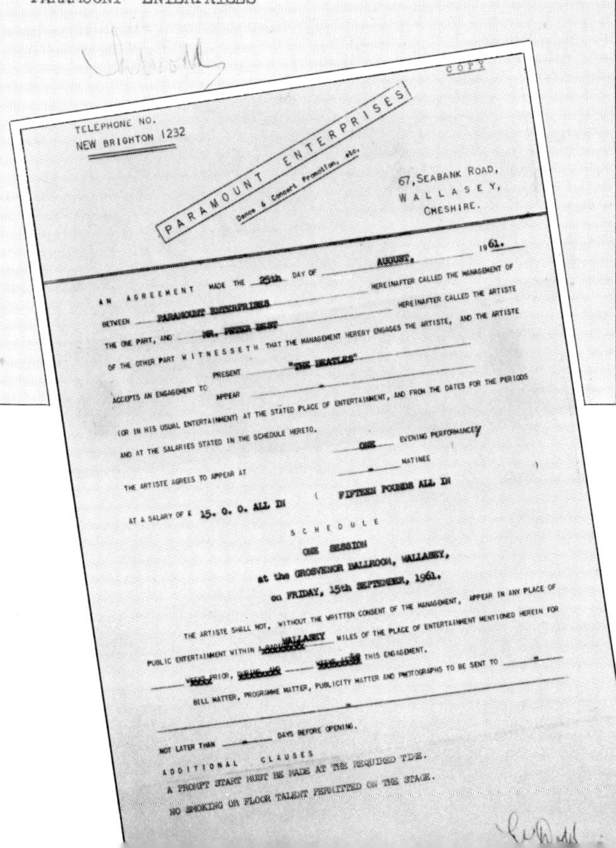

COPY

TELEPHONE NO.
NEW BRIGHTON 1232

PARAMOUNT ENTERPRISES
Dance & Concert Promotion, etc.

67, SEABANK ROAD,
WALLASEY,
CHESHIRE.

AN AGREEMENT MADE THE 25th DAY OF AUGUST, 1961. BETWEEN PARAMOUNT ENTERPRISES HEREINAFTER CALLED THE MANAGEMENT OF THE ONE PART, AND MR. PETER BEST HEREINAFTER CALLED THE ARTISTE OF THE OTHER PART WITNESSETH THAT THE MANAGEMENT HEREBY ENGAGES THE ARTISTE, AND THE ARTISTE ACCEPTS AN ENGAGEMENT TO PRESENT "THE BEATLES" APPEAR — (OR IN HIS USUAL ENTERTAINMENT) AT THE STATED PLACE OF ENTERTAINMENT, AND FROM THE DATES FOR THE PERIODS AND AT THE SALARIES STATED IN THE SCHEDULE HERETO.

THE ARTISTE AGREES TO APPEAR AT ONE EVENING PERFORMANCE — MATINEE

AT A SALARY OF £ 15. 0. 0. ALL IN (FIFTEEN POUNDS ALL IN)

SCHEDULE

ONE SESSION
at the GROSVENOR BALLROOM, WALLASEY,
on FRIDAY, 15th SEPTEMBER, 1961.

THE ARTISTE SHALL NOT, WITHOUT THE WRITTEN CONSENT OF THE MANAGEMENT, APPEAR IN ANY PLACE OF PUBLIC ENTERTAINMENT WITHIN WALLASEY MILES OF THE PLACE OF ENTERTAINMENT MENTIONED HEREIN FOR WEEKS PRIOR, DURING AND THIS ENGAGEMENT.

BILL MATTER, PROGRAMME MATTER, PUBLICITY MATTER AND PHOTOGRAPHS TO BE SENT TO — NOT LATER THAN — DAYS BEFORE OPENING.

ADDITIONAL CLAUSES

A PROMPT START MUST BE MADE AT THE REQUIRED TIME.

NO SMOKING OR FLOOR TALENT PERMITTED ON THE STAGE.

The busy Beatles were now in need of a regular driver or road manager; someone to get us there on time, to attend to the loading and unloading of the accumulating equipment, to lend a hand setting up. There were 101 things to see to and Frank Garner, Mo's bouncer at the Casbah and our part-time driver, was finding it impossible to combine the two jobs, especially at weekends.

I found the answer in Neil Aspinall. He had been an early devotee of the Casbah and had known George and Paul during their schooldays. He became a pal of mine and a friend of the family, so much so that he moved into our home as a guest with a room of his own upstairs. Neil was a trainee-accountant, beavering away at a correspondence course and working days as a ledger clerk, a bright lad with a mind for detail, known as Nel by those close to him, especially the Beatles.

When it became obvious that Frank Garner could no longer cope with looking after us I put the question to Neil: 'Why don't you get yourself a van and cart us around? It'll pay for itself in no time.'

He bought a battered old grey and maroon model for £15 – but at least it went, which was the main consideration. So Neil entered enthusiastically the world of showbusiness as our first roadie. He was right on the spot for the job as well: all the Beatles' kit apart from the guitars was kept at my home.

It included, of course, my drums, which had now taken on a new look. After we had settled down on our return from the Top Ten, I felt it was high time that the group's name should blaze forth from the bass drum. It was a self-imposed 'do-it-yourself' job. This drum was 26ins (66cm) in diameter as against the conventional 24ins (61cm) – and I covered the whole area with flaming orange-red gloss paint which looked like the setting sun and could be seen for about 300 miles! On this glaring background I picked out the word 'BEATLES' in white. It must have looked sickening, but none of us thought so at the time.

Neil's old banger, in which the Beatles travelled cheerfully with all the gear, would be replaced by a shiny new van after the advent of Brian Epstein. Neil would become full-time road manager, and when, at the height of the group's success, Apple Corps Ltd was formed, he would be appointed its managing director. It was to prove a long road for Neil Aspinall.

In September 1961, John, feeling flush with some money sent by an aunt in Scotland, suddenly took off to Paris with Paul for a week's holiday, leaving George and I to fend off broken bookings. It seemed a little odd that they didn't tell us, but I was not too worried. We were a happy-go-lucky bunch and everything was back to normal once the week had passed.

One of the attractions of Paris was that an old 'exi' friend from Hamburg named Jurgen Vollmer was there at the same time, a fact John

Lennon gleaned from the regular and lengthy correspondence he kept up with Stu. Among the topics of conversation with Jurgen the subject of hairstyles must have come up. Jurgen was already a dedicated fringe man himself, so the two Beatles decided at last to follow Stu and George in cultivating the combed-forward fashion which would eventually lead to the Beatles being described universally as mop-tops. Still, on their return, no one suggested that I should fall in line.

Another trend resulted from that holiday in France. On the way John and Paul had stopped off in London; wandering along Charing Cross Road they had been attracted to the windows of Annello and Davide, specialists in ballet and theatrical footwear. Flamenco-style, calf-length black boots with Cuban heels and a tag at the back immediately took Lennon's eye. 'I fell in love with them,' he said, 'and just had to get some.' So did Paul – and so did we all after they swaggered back to Merseyside. George and I ordered them from the same outfitters and they were our pride and joy, worn with our black leather clothes; I would polish my pair for hours. Soon all the Liverpool groups were copying us.

There would be more trends to set. Not very long after the return of John and Paul from Paris, our Svengali in the guise of Brian Epstein, immaculate in his neat city business suit, gingerly poked his wary head into the steaming Cavern one lunchtime just to take a look at four perspiring lads in leather.

Directors: Sidney L. Bernstein, Cecil G. Bernstein, Denis Forman, Maurice King, Victor A. Peers, John S. E. Todd, Joseph Warton, Richard J. Willder.

GRANADA TV NETWORK LIMITED

GRANADA HOUSE WATER STREET MANCHESTER 3
GRANADA MANCHESTER TELEX
DEANSGATE 7211

21st September 1961

Dear Mrs. Best,

Thank you for your letter telling me about "The Beatles". I will certainly bear them in mind and will contact you again if it is possible to invite them to take part in our programme PEOPLE AND PLACES at any time.

Yours sincerely,

David Plowright
Producer

Mrs. M. Best,
8 Hayman's Green,
West Derby,
Liverpool, 12.

DP/AI

Brian Epstein

10

ENTER MR EPSTEIN

The story goes that Brian Epstein first became conscious of our existence when a lad named Raymond Jones ambled into his booming record store in Whitechapel on Saturday, 28 October 1961 and asked to buy a copy of the Beatles' *My Bonnie*, 'made in Germany'. Brian, who was justly proud of his knowledge of current discs and was already reviewing them for Bill Harry in *Mersey Beat*, said he had never heard of it or the Beatles. However, never wishing to disappoint a customer he promised to make some enquiries and scribbled a note to remind himself to 'check on Monday' – by which time two girls had walked into the store with the same request. On the scant information supplied by Raymond Jones our disc would take some tracing. *My Bonnie* billed Tony Sheridan as the lead and we were simply listed as the Beat Brothers; no mention of Beatles.

It seems almost impossible that Brian had no knowledge of us. The Cavern was only a short walk away from Whitechapel and we were appearing several times a week. Since the start of *Mersey Beat* we had been splashed across its pages. Perhaps Brian never read the magazine himself, even though he wrote for it and sold it in his shop. He explained the lapse later by saying that Mersey rock had not been his scene (he preferred orchestral music, with a particular leaning towards Sibelius) and that, being 27, he was not of the right age-group, although he did recall in his autobiography, *A Cellarful of Noise*, that he had once seen our name on a poster advertising an appearance at a dance in New Brighton.

On the other hand, we knew of Epstein. We used to loaf around his North End Music Stores (NEMS) shop in our leathers, listening to the latest American releases but rarely buying them. I found out that it was one of the girls we used to chat up at NEMS when Epstein wasn't looking who eventually told him that we were local lads who could be found just round the corner at the Cavern.

There was no great excitement on our part when at one lunchtime session early in November Bob Wooler announced that Brian Epstein was out there somewhere in the sea of faces and would the audience give him a big hand. Brian had asked Bill Harry to smooth his entry into the unknown that was the Cavern and Wooler had been expecting him.

Epstein watched us with some interest, noting (with some distaste as he revealed later) that we were scruffy, loutish, thumping each other and even eating on stage. Intent on his search for *My Bonnie*, at the end of a set he braved his way forward through the sweat and dandruff towards the stage and managed to have a word with George Harrison, explaining his quest. The record was produced from the little bandroom and played for him. (It was Paul's presentation copy of the disc that Bob Wooler used to spin; I still have mine at home.) Epstein noted the details, but the rest of us didn't meet him on that occasion.

He was later to confess that he had felt strangely drawn to us, despite the age gap and contrasting background. He was a former public schoolboy (from the Wrekin School), and heir to the family furniture and record store business which owned two shops in the city. He soon paid the Cavern another visit and again it was George who passed on to us a personal message that this shy, immaculately-dressed chap would like to see us in his office after we were through. He thought he might be able to help us.

It was a Wednesday at the beginning of December, an early-closing day when NEMS shut for the afternoon. We had a few pints in the Grapes in Mathew Street first, then strolled on to see him afterwards, taking our time and arriving later than he expected us.

Brian opened up to let us in and we just stared vacantly at him. We had eyed each other so many times before at NEMS, where we used to crowd into the booths, cadging a listen to the latest discs by the Shirelles, Bobby Vee, Marvin Gaye and others. Whenever he discovered us, bunched together playing record after record, one of us would quickly grab a disc, crying, 'That's the one. Who's buying?' He would just glare at us, knowing we had no intention of making a purchase.

Now we stood there in very different circumstances – sheepish and untidy and late, but Epstein made an effort to put us at our ease. He was obviously shy, but he smiled and welcomed us inside. Upstairs in his office he said, tongue-in-cheek: 'I used to dread you people coming in, completely disrupting the place.' Then he went on to explain the purpose of the visit. 'I'm the manager of this store,' he said, 'and I think I can do something for you.'

'Can you buy us into the charts, Brian?' Lennon asked mischievously.

Brian played along. 'No' he smiled, 'but I think I can do a lot for you.' He had apparently checked up on us contractually and found that we managed our own affairs, for he went on to say that he would like to manage us. 'I'll be quite honest,' he admitted, 'I've never been engaged in this kind of thing before.'

There were some moments of silence, then Lennon said to me: 'What do you think?'

'We'll have to talk it over,' I said. I didn't consider myself to be manager of the Beatles, although I dealt with all our business matters. I was *acting* manager and it wouldn't break my heart to shed the administrative load, but Brian's offer wasn't one to decide all in a few moments. Lennon seemed to be in agreement. 'We'll let you know,' he told Epstein and we said our goodbyes and left, promising to be in touch.

Certainly there were several things in his favour, most of them connected with the fact that Eppy – as he would be known to us from now on – was well-heeled.

'See the suit he'd got on?' said George, impressed.

'And the shiny shoes,' someone else put in. But we all agreed he was a bit 'antwakky', a bit of Liverpool dialect that meant Mr Epstein was pretty out of step as far as we were concerned. Even so, we concluded he was a neat gentleman indeed, he even carried a briefcase with him into the Cavern. But it was the general opinion of the Beatles that we could change him – he wouldn't change us.

We each discussed this new direction in our lives with our 'elders and betters', although I can't be certain if John consulted Aunt Mimi. Anyway, he was now 21, having reached his majority on 9 October, so could do what he liked. As for the rest of us, our parents were in no doubt that Brian Epstein could be good for us. For our part the attraction was the possibility that he could be more positive in widening our horizon. We were nearing our zenith on Merseyside and faced the prospect of being stuck there unless we could somehow break through on a national basis. London was the recording company Mecca and we needed to get aboard a British label if we were ever to escape the Liverpool-Hamburg shuttle service. Eppy was in the record business; he would know people; and he had promised to help.

Mo recalls today that at that time she thought Brian could only be good for us. 'He was so keen and full of enthusiasm,' she says. 'He was also young and certainly seemed to be the type of person who could do something for the Beatles. I had tried to help them as much as I could along the way and perhaps now he might be able to push them along further. I could see nothing but stardom ahead for the group. They were fantastic!'

It must have been the following Friday when we bundled off to NEMS once more after the usual tanking up in the Grapes. The shop was open this time, of course, and we scurried first into the record department to survey the latest hits, before making our way upstairs (where they sold washing machines, TV sets and pianos) and through to Brian's office.

Left: Pete Best

Above: The Beatles at the Cavern in 1961, at the time Brian Epstein became their manager.

Right: Fans queueing outside the Cavern.

We first were confronted by a girl assistant who appeared somewhat startled. 'We'd like to see Mr Epstein, please,' we said. Yes, we did say please. Even so she looked at us with some little doubt. Four rockers to see her well-groomed, well-spoken boss? It obviously didn't seem possible. 'We do have an appointment,' we told her.

After she had buzzed him on the phone we trooped in and once more stood before him in an embarrassing silence until Lennon blurted out our verdict.

'Okay, you're on!' he said.

'Do you really mean it?' Eppy asked with a blush.

'We're in business,' John said, and the rest of us mouthed some kind of approval.

It took a few moments for the decision to sink in. Then, businesslike, Brian said: 'The first thing is a contract. It'll take quite a time to draw up, but I can take it that I'm now the manager?' We all said yes – and kow-towed like four pilgrims paying their homage towards Mecca. Eppy put on a sly grin.

The next time we saw him was at the Cavern. When he had called there before, he had kept a respectful distance. This time we invited him into the holy of holies – the cramped bandroom.

'Meet our manager!' we said to Bob Wooler, who was sorting his DJ records and had known earlier of Brian's offer. 'Welcome to the sanctum,' said Bob.

Eppy edged into the room, looking very shy and not a little out of place. He sat down nervously on the first bench, which meant he was visible to the audience. Beads of perspiration began to form on his forehead as he breathed in disinfectant fumes. It really wasn't a place for a fellow who might have just stepped out of a tailor's window, but in his shy way he would get used to the Cavern. Catching a glimpse of him on the off-stage bench, fans wondered 'Who's the dapper fellow?' They soon learned the answer. It wasn't long before he was explaining to everybody, with a touch of pride, that he was our manager. We eased him into the scene, but none too gently. 'Brian!' we would say, 'let's go and buy some Cokes at the back – you're the manager!' And he would do as he was told, cheerfully, trying hard to be one of the boys in this strange new world of sweat, rock and Cuban heels.

He would be there with us at all times during these very busy days. We would play the Cavern one night and on another the Iron Door, a rival club to the Cavern, also situated in an old warehouse some two or three hundred yards away. It, too, had been a venue for trad jazz, but there the similarities ended. The Iron Door was fresh with new paint and minus 'dandruff' in the basement where the groups played.

If anyone wanted to know what a nice guy like Brian was doing in places like these he readily announced that he was our manager, still with some diffidence. He would even sit it out with us at the all-night sessions the Cavern occasionally put on, usually at Bank Holiday times. The fun ran from seven in the evening till seven next morning and there might be a dozen or more groups taking part.

The news that he had taken us under his wing spread round Liverpool like a prairie fire. The name meant something to a lot of people and clearly he commanded respect. 'You're going places now,' was a frequent comment. We signed the deal confirming Brian as manager in the sitting room at Hayman's Green above the Casbah, which would still remain the group headquarters. As three of us were still under 21, the contract had to be witnessed. Performing this duty was Alastair Taylor, who then worked in Brian's store but later would rise in the NEMS empire to be general manager.

Our signatures were scrawled across the Queen's head on sixpenny stamps. John Winston Lennon (in 1969 he would change it to John Ono Lennon in an official rooftop ceremony at the Apple Corps headquarters in London) ... James Paul McCartney ... Peter Randolph Best (so the contract described me, transposing my Christian names, although I signed it R.P. Best) ... and plain George Harrison. I never have seen mention of a middle name for George.

Only one stamp failed to accommodate a signature – the first and most important on the document: the one reserved for Brian Epstein. Nevertheless, he would say in his book later, 'I abided by the terms and no one worried.' Certainly no one worried on that day, but we did wonder later if Brian had been scared to sign for some reason, perhaps in case anything went embarrassingly wrong and he would be held responsible.

At the outset he used me as a sort of leaning post, which led to a friendship with him and a closer relationship than he had with the other three. I found him shrewd, but extremely raw in his knowledge of our business and immature when it came to handling a group such as the Beatles. No doubt because I had been our administrator before he happened along, he seemed to be able to communicate with me on a more serious level, frequently discussing deals and the future of the group. He also sought advice from the ever-willing Bob Wooler.

Sometimes Epstein joined us over drinks at the Grapes, where our usual was a Brown Mix – mild and brown ale – or Guinness and cider, which we called Black Velvet. Brian drank brandy and we nicknamed him the Brandyman, as well as Eppy.

It was apparent that he didn't really know how to react to us in those early days. He wasn't actually scared, but he was always extremely polite, prefixing every request with 'could we...' or 'would it be possible...' He treated us with the utmost respect and would probably have been told to 'bugger off' if he hadn't. But he did show from the

LEWIS BUCKLEY ENTERTAINMENTS LTD.

Directors: Lewis Buckley, Vera F. Buckley

28 CARR LANE,
BIRKDALE,
SOUTHPORT,
LANCASHIRE

SOUTHPORT 77141-2

5th September, 1961.

PD

The Beatles,
C/o The Cavern Jazz Club,
10 Mathew Street,
LIVERPOOL.

Dear Sirs,

I would appreciate details of your vacant Saturdays during the next two months and fees required to appear at Northwich and Crewe.

Would you also kindly give details of instrumentation.

Yours sincerely,

start that he could be tough and would be very annoyed if anyone turned up late for a date. Early on in our association, Paul was missing from one afternoon business meeting with Eppy. George rang the McCartney home only to discover that Paul was taking a bath before setting out. Brian was furious at Paul's off-hand attitude, and, glancing angrily at his watch, said: 'Paul's going to be very late!' 'But very clean!' George remarked, so even Eppy had to smile.

Gradually we learned more about his background; about his family and how his grandfather had arrived in Britain as a Polish immigrant; of how Brian himself had been called up into the Army as a National Serviceman for two years but was home again within a year, discharged on medical grounds; of how he had ambitions as an actor and had studied at the Royal Academy of Dramatic Art in London, but had left, disenchanted with the theatrical life, and had settled back in Liverpool to play his part in the family business instead.

We began to hear stories that he was homosexual and had been the 'Mr X' in some homosexual court case. (Homosexuality was still totally illegal in those days.) I believe he didn't have the courage to tell us that he was one; not that it would have made any difference if he had. More important was knowing that he was a man ready to dedicate himself to us and to our future.

He could be our ticket to the Big Time, which is why we went along – under some protest – with his suggestions that we smarten up; that we should discard our 'German' look for neat suits. He claimed that no one in the world of entertainment outside our present environment would tolerate our slovenly look, our chatting to the birds near the stage, our eating and drinking on the stand, our playful butting and jostling and generally enjoying ourselves. Discipline was what we needed most; perhaps Brian's brief term in the Army had inspired him, along with his own fastidious tastes. Lennon was more reluctant to change than the rest of us and told Brian so in his best caustic manner. But in the end we all conformed.

Our first stage suits were shiny dark blue mohair which had been purchased for our first night club date in Liverpool's Cabaret Club, an engagement arranged by Epstein. This was an up-market venue and not the kind of place we had been used to. Lennon was in rebellious mood, already having voiced the opinion that our new manager was trying to turn us into Little Lord Fauntleroys.

When John saw the club's multi-coloured check flooring he could contain himself no longer: 'How the hell can you expect us to perform in shiny bloody suits on a floor like that?' he stormed at Eppy. 'With all the lights and reflection we'll look like bloody rainbows!'

Brian blushed the way he always would, clenching his fists until his knuckles showed white.

Hamming it up at the Cavern: George, John and Pete collect, while Paul fakes a death bed scene.

THE ZODIACS

posite and above: Rocking it up on stage at the Cavern. Below: The Beatles with American soul singer Davy Jones, earsing his latest hit at the Cavern. They backed him at several Liverpool gigs, including one at the Cavern that same ning.

'You just manage us – don't try to redesign us!' John went on relentlessly. 'People want to see the Beatles! This isn't the Beatles!' Which was true: we were at home in our leathers; we liked to be casual. Suits and collars and ties were for people who worked in offices.

Lennon's outburst made no difference. When hurt, Brian retired from such scenes as this in silence, and we went on wearing our suits – four up-market looking lads playing for up-market people. And we would go on wearing suits – and ties.

At this time Brian had another worry – that we shouldn't become involved with drugs of any kind. There were so many stories of jazz and pop musicians being charged with drug offences and they caused him concern. This was not for the Beatles, he said firmly. This was no way to the top and, in one of his impassioned pep talks, he implored us to steer clear.

My friendship with Epstein continued during this period of change as he became more absorbed in the business. He even took me out to his family home in the smart suburb of Childwall to meet his father Harry and his mother Queenie. I was there for about half an hour and found it all very pleasant, without detecting any hint that his interest in me might be anything other than businesslike. But it did happen.

We were having drinks after a lunchtime Cavern session when he asked me if I would mind if he called for me and took me for a drive that evening. It was a night when the Beatles were without an engagement, so we set off in Brian's smart Ford Zodiac, talking mainly about business, as we frequently did in his office.

Blackpool lay ahead as he said: 'I have a very fond admiration of you.'

'Me or the group?' I asked him, a bit confused. He made it clear that he meant me personally.

We had reached the outskirts of the resort when he came to the point. 'Pete,' he said, 'would you find it embarrassing if I ask you to stay in a hotel overnight? I'd like to spend the night with you.'

It didn't sound terribly shocking at the time, the way the question had been put and I admit that I didn't immediately realize that I was being propositioned. I hadn't experienced anything like this before. I told him that I would much prefer to go home, which we did. There was no argument, no scene.

In retrospect it was obvious that he had wanted to start a relationship, but there had been nothing nasty about it, nothing obscene, nothing dirty. It was a very gentle approach. He never again asked me to go for a drive with him and never returned to the subject of a relationship. We both carefully forgot about the journey to Blackpool and the conversation of that night.

Epstein immersed himself in the problem of trying to find a major record company that might be interested in his new charges, and astonished us by the pace at which he worked. Just before Christmas 1961, Brian, using his contacts and his muscle as a major record retailer in the north-west, had intrigued the Decca company sufficiently to induce them to send a scout from London to take a look at these Beatles who were the rage of Merseyside.

The Decca scout was a young chap named Mike Smith, who had been lending an ear to talent on behalf of his boss, Dick Rowe, head of the all-important Artists and Repertoire (A&R) department of the recording giant, which marketed a host of American as well as home-produced hits. During his long career, Dick had been associated with a string of household names, ranging from big bands to star singers.

Mike Smith braved the rigours of the Cavern to listen to us and liked what he had heard. After his return to London word came quickly that Decca wanted us to audition for them. The date was set for 1 January 1962. It was some way to start a New Year.

JIM GRETTY

presents

STAR MATINEE

with your compere ARTHUR SCOTT introducing . . .

1. The Dusty Road Ramblers
2. Les Arnold
3. Joe Cordova
4. Dunn and Markey
5. Bob McGrady
6. Lennie Rens
7. Shirley Gordon
8. Bert King
9. The Eltones
10. The Beatles
11. Dennis Horton and Gladys Ambrose
12. Jackie Owen and the Joe Royal Trio
13. Edna Bell
14. Jim Gretty
15. Denis Smerdon
16. KEN DODD

an—BERT SMITH

Ley and Joe Royal

George Martin and Jim Gretty

Programme for 'The Ken Dodd Show' – the Beatles opened the second half of the Liverpool comedian's showcase variety show on October 15, 1960.

OPERATION

'Big Beat'

TOWER BALLROOM

NEW BRIGHTON

Friday, 10TH Nov. 1961

7·30 P.M. to 1·0 A.M.

★ *Rocking to Merseysides* TOP 5 GROUPS

The Beatles

Rory Storm and the Hurricanes

Gerry & The Pacemakers

The Remo Four

Kingsize Taylor and the Dominoes

2 LICENSED BARS (until 11·30 P.M.) BUFFET

Special Late Transport (L,POOL · WIRRAL · CHESHIRE)

TICKETS 5/- from RUSHWORTHS · LEWIS'S
CRANES · STOTHERS
TOWER BALLROOM

The Beatles backing Davy Jones at the Tower Ballroom, New Brighton, on December 8, 1960.

The Beatles' set during 'The Davy Jones Show' at the Tower Ballroom, New Brighton. Inset right: Paul takes the mike for a solo ballad; above and below: entrance tickets for 'Big Beat Sessions' and 'The Davy Jones Show'.

The Davy Jones Show

TOWER BALLROOM, NEW BRIGHTON

FRIDAY, 8th DECEMBER 1961

7-30 p.m. to 1-00 a.m.

Presenting America's Top 'Beat' Entertainer—Reprise Recording Artiste

the Great **Davy Jones**

Co-Starring The Latest Singing Sensation

Danny Williams

Hit Recorder of "Moon River" (Theme of "Breakfast at Tiffanys")

also The Beatles - - - - Rory Storm and The Hurricanes

Gerry and The Pacemakers - - - - The Remo Fou

Earl Preston and The T.Ts. - - - - The Big Th

Licensed Bars (until 11-30 p.m.)

LATE TRANSPORT (Liverpool, Wirral and Cheshire)

Excursions Leaving St. John's Lane (Lime Street) 7-30 p.m. to

TICKETS 7/6

BIG BEAT SESSIONS

EVERY FRIDAY at the

TOWER BALLROOM, NEW BRIGHTON

FRIDAY, 1st DECEMBER 1961

Another Great Six Band Line Up -

THE BEATLES - - RORY STORM AND THE HURRICANES
DALE ROBERTS AND THE JAYWALKERS - DERRY AND THE SENIORS
KINGSIZE TAYLOR & THE DOMINOES - STEVE DAY & THE DRIFTERS

First Heat "Mr. Twist" Competition

7-30 p.m. to 1-00 a.m. Licensed Bars (until 11-30 p.m.)

LATE TRANSPORT (Liverpool, Wirral and Cheshire)

Excursions Leaving St. John's Lane (Lime Street) 7-30 p.m. to 9-00 p.m.

TICKETS 4/6

Sweating it out in a good cause: Brian Epstein introduces composer Lionel Bart (left) to the Cavern Club.

11

DEALS AND DISAPPOINTMENTS

Brian Epstein already had his selling line: 'I've got four boys who are going to be bigger than Elvis!' He would say it to recording companies, to pressmen, to anybody showing some interest in the new, cleaned-up version of the Beatles. It must have sounded laughable at the time. Elvis was sitting firmly on his throne, having succeeded Bill Haley years back as the King of Rock'n'Roll. The world lay before him and from where we sat he appeared to be immovable.

We had often discussed our ambitions and we knew the first objective was to record for a major label and top the charts. Elvis was light years away in our reckoning. Yet all four of us were convinced that one day the Beatles would be famous. We felt that we had a certain charisma, a special relationship with audiences, though we never tried to guess just how far success might take us. We saw no further than a Number One record. We had a sort of chant which John used to lead: 'Where are we going, lads?' he would yell. 'To the toppermost of the poppermost!' was our shouted reply.

On New Year's Eve, 1961, however, there were no thoughts of being bigger than anyone as we headed for London. We travelled down without Brian, who was due to meet us at the Decca studios next morning. It was bitterly cold and it was snowing; Neil Aspinall drove us down by van and the journey took up most of the day. In the Midlands he lost his way in the snow, and the revellers were already about in London's West End by the time we booked into the Royal Hotel near Russell Square. Instead of an early-to-bed night we decided to join the New Year festivities in Trafalgar Square and watch all those daft lads jump into the fountain and dance in the spray as we had seen in previous years on television.

We had a few beers in a pub near Charing Cross while Neil parked the van. When he joined us he was full of excitement. Two fellows had approached him and asked if they could climb into the van for a few minutes. It was some seconds before he realized they were junkies looking for somewhere to give themselves a fix, but once he had they were told to 'bugger off'.

In the square we joined in the singing of *Auld Lang Syne*, kissed a few willing lips but we didn't exactly let ourselves rip, and we didn't even dip as much as a finger into the icy waters of the fountains, where the usual bravehearts were trying to catch pneumonia. The implications of the audition were uppermost in our minds; at last the Big Time was beckoning. Decca was a name known throughout the world and we had to be ready to take them by storm in the morning.

It certainly wasn't a good start to New Year's Day, however. We were due to meet Eppy at the studios at 10.30am but didn't arrive until around eleven. I can't remember whether we overslept or were held up in London's traffic – 1 January was not a public holiday at that time so it was business as usual in the city. Brian was really angry. He always made a point of being punctual himself and couldn't abide other people being late. He had also been understandably worried. 'I had visions of you being smashed up in the van,' he said, obviously relieved at seeing us in one piece.

Mike Smith, who was to conduct the audition, welcomed us in the studio and we tried to put a bold face on the drama that was about to unfold. 'Happy New Year, Mike,' George said, 'didn't see you in the fountain last night!' But most of us were already suffering from nerves.

For the first time in our lives we were in a top-flight studio and felt the thrill of it, contrasting its sophistication with the barren school hall in Hamburg in which we cut *My Bonnie*. In the midst of Decca's electronic splendour our amps must have appeared rather shabby, for they insisted that we took advantage of their equipment instead. Our nervousness showed during some of the takes, mostly during the solo voices, but we ploughed on from midday until well into the afternoon, giving of our best.

Eppy and Mike Smith chose a mixture of songs that they calculated would have the Decca bigwigs standing on their heads. Among them were *The Sheik Of Araby*, *Till There Was You*, *Take Good CAre of My Baby*, *Money*, *Memphis Tennessee*, *Three Cool Cats* and *September In The Rain*. I believe there were two Lennon-McCartney efforts – *Like Dreamers Do* and a new composition of Paul's called *Love Of The Loved*. Thinking back, it was a strange dish to set before the recording kings, with the emphasis on standards which, I remember, was mainly at Brian's insistence. Really we were doing little that was different.

Only one sour note marred the proceedings. At one stage Brian began to voice some criticism either of John's singing or his guitar playing, I'm not sure which. Lennon burst into one of his bouts of violent, uncontrollable temper, during which his face would alternate from white to red.

'You've got nothing to do with the music!' he raged at Eppy. 'You go back and count your money, you Jewish git!'

Brian looked like he had cracked down the middle; he blushed profusely, seething inside but remaining silent. Everything stopped. Mike Smith, the sound engineers and the rest of us all looked at each other in amazement. Then Epstein walked out and didn't return for nearly twenty minutes.

We could hardly wait to hear the play-backs and when we did listen to the results we were well pleased. Mike Smith and Eppy, now recovered from John's outburst, also seemed to be extremely happy with the way the session had gone. All that was left was the verdict from on high, but that wouldn't be given immediately. Eppy was optimistic enough to treat us all to a spanking dinner before we began the drive home; we went to a restaurant at Swiss Cottage recommended by Mike Smith. Everybody was in high spirits, convinced that the audition had been a great success and that stardom was lurking just around the corner, and no one was more jubilant than Brian. He had driven down to London on his own, but he had company on the return journey, as Paul and George opted for the comfort of his Zodiac while John and I joined Neil in the van.

Then came the long wait. We felt certain that we would hear the good news from Decca within a few days, but they dragged past into a week, then another week and another until they stretched into months. All the initial enthusiasm wore thin and our hopes began to fade a little more with each week of silence. Brian had lost his ready smile and badgered Decca for a decision.

It wasn't until March that he learned from top man Dick Rowe we had been given the thumbs down. According to Eppy, Dick had told him 'groups of guitarists are on the way out', to which Brian trotted out his slogan that one day we were going to be bigger than Elvis, which he still fervently believed.

Brian returned from London with the sad news late at night and at Lime Street Station apparently rang one of the other Beatles to gather the rest of the group to meet him. I wasn't invited and, puzzlingly, the news of the Decca turn-down was kept from me for days to come. When I did eventually learn our fate their lame excuse was that they had all thought I would take the result extremely badly. I had to laugh in my bewilderment.

What kind of a guy did they take me for? I had roared and rampaged through Hamburg with them, gone mugging with John and waded into all sorts of thugs with him. What had changed to make any one of them think I might be broken up by this particular kick in the pants? My reaction was as normal as their own. It wasn't the end of the world for the Beatles.

Best Wishes

As for Dick Rowe, he became The Man Who Turned Down The Beatles for ever more – the title he chose when he decided to write his autobiography recently. 'More people know me for that reason rather than for any successes I have had – because of Brian Epstein's vindictiveness,' he told Patrick Doncaster in a 1980 interview for the *Daily Mirror*. He was the only record company boss actually named in Brian's own book as rejecting the Beatles, although at least four other major companies would also turn us down after listening to our demo tapes.

'I wasn't even present when the Beatles auditioned for Decca,' Rowe said. 'I heard only the tapes they recorded. They sounded out of tune to me, but I had been told that they were very nervous. They played mostly old standard tunes.'

Dick also recalled that Mike Smith had auditioned a London-based group, Brian Poole and the Tremeloes, and that economics had played their part in our rejection. It was cheaper to experiment with the Tremeloes rather than have us trekking to and from Liverpool, so Brian Poole got the Decca thumbs up and went on to make hit records that caused a mere ripple compared with the giant waves that the Beatles would eventually make.

Saying no to the Beatles did have one compensation for Dick Rowe. Much later he happened to be in Liverpool as a talent show judge along with George Harrison. 'George,' Dick told him, 'I've really got a sore arse from turning you lot down.' George replied that Mr Rowe might be doing himself a favour if he popped into the Station Hotel at Richmond in Surrey some weekend to catch a group calling themselves the Rolling Stones; Rowe did ... and put them on record.

I came by a pirated copy of the Decca audition tape years later through a guy I know in New York. It didn't sound all that bad; I particularly admire *Like Dreamers Do*. Today the tape has been released legitimately as an album called *Silver Beatles* – cleaned up and much improved soundwise.

Of all of us, I feel Epstein was most dejected after the news from Decca, but he continued to strive for us and bombarded the other companies with Beatles tapes. But the answer would prove to be the same. Pye would say no to us. Philips would say no. Two of the best-known labels in the EMI complex – HMV and Columbia – would both say no.

Meantime there were a couple of bright specks to lighten the horizon. One was our first broadcast for the BBC, which resulted from our having topped the *Mersey Beat* popularity poll. The programme was called 'Play Hour', I think; it was recorded before an audience in the Playhouse Theatre in Manchester during the afternoon, for broadcast later the same evening.

Previous page: a curtain-call for leather; the last photo-session featuring the Beatles in Hamburg black.

Paul's father travelled with us to Manchester, where we appeared spick and span in our mohair suits. On stage we were introduced individually to a fantastic reception from some 300 to 400 girls, which led *Mersey Beat* to comment later: 'John, Paul and George made their entrance on stage to cheers and applause, but when Pete walked on – the fans went wild! The girls screamed. In Manchester his popularity was assured by his looks alone.'

As we tried to leave the theatre after the broadcast there was another demonstration of the onward march of Beatlemania. It wasn't simply a case of being mobbed; they came at us like a pack of hounds – girls, girls, girls. I was last in line as we tried to fight our way through to our transport home, and I caught the worst of it. John, Paul and George struggled on, but suddenly I found myself trapped. I lost tuffs of hair and my tie. The new mohair suit took a terrific mauling and was all but ripped off. Struggling girls surrounded me with autograph books while dozens more were passed over the sea of heads in the hope of a signature as I stood there unable to move in any direction.

Paul's father watched the whole frantic scene and wasn't very pleased at what he saw. When I finally escaped he came up to me and said sourly: 'Why did you have to attract all the attention? Why didn't you call the other lads back?' I told him there was nothing I could have done. I was trapped and had to literally fight for my life to get out. If I could have found a way through I certainly would have done so. His comment was: 'I think that was very selfish of you.' Later I reported the conversation to Eppy and he promised to talk to Jim McCartney about the incident. I don't know if he ever did.

That night, I listened to the recorded broadcast with Paul at my house before we went to play the Cavern; we both thought it sounded great. At the club Bob Wooler added a new dimension to his introduction. 'As well as recording stars,' he said, 'stars of radio! Now see them in person. Your hometown lads! Your own Beatles!'

The second bright speck on our horizon was a plum third residency in Hamburg for seven weeks starting on 13 April. It was really something to look forward to while the recording bosses in London had nothing to offer but a shake of the head.

Before flying off we gave some farewell shows, including one at the Casbah which I particularly remember. Epstein arrived wearing a leather jacket, polo sweater and Cuban heels! 'For Chrissake!' Lennon exploded. 'Look! Changes us into suits and now he wants to be one of us!'

Eppy blushed red, clenched his fists and was silent for some seconds. Then very politely he said: 'Well, it's casual, isn't it?'

Three days before our Hamburg residency was due to start, John, Paul and I flew out together without George, who was recovering from

German measles; he was due to follow us out in a day or so with Brian. We were in buoyant mood as the plane tucked up its wheels and continued to climb. We were on our way to open Hamburg's newest and most prestigious night spot, the Star Club, a lavish new enterprise in our old stamping ground, the Grosse Freiheit; this time we would have our own flat, complete with a balcony.

This was recognition indeed: top billing in the number one venue, somewhere pleasant to rest our heads and a pay packet of about £100 a week each. We could afford to feel happy when the aircraft began its approach and the order came to fasten seat belts. Stu Sutcliffe and Astrid would be waiting to greet us; we had seen them a couple of times since our tearful parting in Hamburg the previous year. They had flown across to Liverpool and there had been brief reunions; they would come and see us perform at a venue and stay and chat afterwards just like the old times. So we were all smiles as we caught sight of Astrid at the airport, standing there alone. It was no surprise that she was dressed in black – she always had done – and of course, she was as pale as ever.

'Where's Stu?' we all wanted to know, expecting that he was ordering the beers or Cokes or maybe simply taking a leak.

Astrid found difficulty mustering the words. 'Stu is dead!' she managed to whisper.

'Dead?' It was unbelievable. Not Stu. Not this little ex-Beatle with magic in his artistic fingers, the really shy one who used to try to cover up his inexperience on bass guitar by looking the other way; the miniature James Dean who had sung so lovingly to Astrid in the audience. Not Stu. We didn't want to believe it.

Tortured for weeks by maddening pains in his head, he had died in Astrid's arms just the day before. We were all deeply affected and didn't try to hide the tears welling into our eyes. John, who had been closer to Stu than Paul or me, wept like a child. I had never seen him break down in public like this before. He had cried his fair share when we had last said farewell to Hamburg, but this was different. He was absolutely shattered.

John could be the hard man we all knew so well; violent and abrasive. But he could be as sentimental and emotional as anyone when something really hurt him – and the tragic news that came from Astrid's pale lips utterly floored him. He had immense respect for Stu's talents as an artist and since Stu's departure from the group their friendship had been kept alive by the lengthy letters, frequently of 30 pages or more, John used to pen to him; pages punctuated with his whacky verse and outrageous cartoons. But now it was all over. Death, in the guise of a tumour on the brain, had claimed its first Beatle at the age of 21.

Right and overleaf: The new look; on Brian Epstein's orders, the Beatles pose (uncomfortably) for the first time in mohair suits.

Star-Club

GRÜSSE AUS DEM Star-Club HAMBURG

12

STARS AT THE STAR CLUB

We were miserable for days as we settled into our new quarters in the Grosse Freiheit across the street from the Star Club. Fortunately its completion had been slightly delayed and we had three or four days to ourselves until it was ready for the grand Beatle opening.

The club was certainly luxurious, spacious, with a balcony that was a relic of its days as a cinema. A false ceiling of trellis-work festooned with lanterns was suspended across the auditorium to reduce the height and create an illusion of club intimacy. There was a proper stage, with curtains which could be pulled across; dressing rooms were spacious, too, and at last we felt that we were receiving star treatment. Of course there were bars as well, and there to attract the males – including the Beatles, naturally – was a bevy of beautiful barmaids.

The man who had planned to transform the premises into a showcase for top American names as well as British, was one Manfred Weissleder, another wide-chested German with reddish hair and a ruddy complexion, who owned a string of St Pauli strip clubs and had founded his fortune on sex. He was one more in the line of big guys that nobody would want to tangle with, but his chief troubleshooter turned out to be our old friend Horst Fascher, who had quit the Top Ten, and was now standing by with his henchmen to quell any disruption in the new set-up.

While we awaited George's arrival a song was born that would have far-reaching consequences for us all. The title started out as *Love, Love Me Do* but was quickly abbreviated by popular agreement by lopping off the first 'love'. The number was conceived in the course of one afternoon in our flat opposite the club; it was a Lennon-McCartney original.

When we gave it a first work-out during two days of rehearsal at the club prior to opening night, somehow it didn't sound right. We would all take part in discussions on how a number should be arranged and we knew that there was something missing from the way *Love Me Do* originally emerged.

Inset left: A post-card view of the Star Club, Hamburg's premier rock and pop venue in 1962.

Influenced by Bruce Channel's hit *Hey! Baby*, which was dominated by harmonica, John began playing around with a new harmonica intro for *Love Me Do*, finally finding the answer in a blues-like wail. It gave the song a hint of sadness, noted by listeners when they heard it later in the year; it was understandable since we were still numbed by Stu's death. Be that as it may, the harmonica strengthened the number considerably, probably helping it on its way to the charts when it became the Beatles' British debut disc.

Our first night at the Star Club was one to remember, with a thunderous reception and well-wishes from old friends. The club was clearly going to be the 'in place' from now on, taking over from Peter Eckhorn's Top Ten. (Peter had wanted us back at the same time, but had been outbid by Weissleder.)

On that opening night Horst Fascher brought us the news that Weissleder wanted to mark the occasion by giving us a present. 'We'll have a Cadillac – or maybe a Mercedes will do!' we joked, all chipping in with ludicrous suggestions. After the first set Weissleder made the presentation backstage in his halting English. We each received a fashionable gold indentity bracelet with our Christian names engraved on one side and 'Star Club' on the reverse.

Mine wouldn't last long. These bracelets hung loose on the wrist and I had to leave mine off whenever I was at the drums. Usually I could slip it into a pocket for safety, but one night following the Hamburg tour we were playing at the Majestic Ballroom in Birkenhead, wearing stage suits without pockets, designed to eliminate any unsightly bulges. I left the bracelet in my everyday trousers in the dressing room; when I came off stage it had vanished.

Meanwhile, in Hamburg, life gradually began to return to normal after Stu's death, although Astrid's presence was a constant reminder. She would come to the Star Club along with friends, putting on a brave face, trying to pick up the threads of her own life but clearly still deeply saddened.

We returned to the endless round of booze and birds. The Star Club was good 'turkin' ground', a phrase derived from 'turkey' and 'stuffing', meaning a venue where girls were readily available. The barmaids especially saw to it that we never felt under-privileged in this respect.

One of these was Bettina, a lovable big-busted baby with a beehive hairdo, who more or less adopted us. Her sole ambition seemed to be to try to pair us off with the other girls. You would need an auditor to calculate the exact number of barmaids and other girls who passed through the doors at our handy apartment. We used to finish our last set around 4am, then our night's fun began.

It was like a swap-shop for birds, with Bettina acting as our fixer. 'No wonder you boys look so happy,' she would smile. But she never indulged with us herself, so developed into a great mate, even accompanying us on our regular Sunday morning excursions to the Fish Market, a ritual we carried on for nearly two years.

Bettina had her own brand of fun. When we gathered at her bar she would put her chin on the counter down between her giant boobs – and then she'd wrap them around our ears! It was a nice way to go deaf for a few seconds. She had her special request numbers that we had to play for her on stage. A dozen lanterns hung above her bar and she would pass along chiming each of them until they were all swinging. 'Now for Bettina!' she would cry. When the number was over she would swing the lanterns again in acknowledgement.

Only one happening – there is no other word for it – ever slowed thelong procession of girls to our den of inquity: it was 'The Thing', and it was George Harrison's fault.

One night, after some excessive drinking along with the rest of us, he was sick on the floor at the side of his bed. This was nothing terribly unusual after a skinful; it was typical of us all. What was different was that next morning he left the mess for the cleaning lady to deal with. She protested that it was not part of her daily duties and it could stay where it was. The trouble was, George decided it wasn't his duty either and she stormed off in the direction of Herr Weissleder in a Teutonic rage.

It wasn't the first time she had complained about the untidy Beatles, whose sweaty socks, discarded clothing, bottles and other items usually littered the place. This fresh contribution from George was the last straw.

In an effort to placate the old lady, Weissleder despatched Horst Fascher to our quarters with an order to George to remove the offending vomit himself. But George became really shirty. It wasn't his job, it could stay where it was for all he cared, even though he had to climb over it to get into bed.

None of this was really typical of George. He rarely involved himself in any sort of argument and was much quieter than the rest of us in those formative days and, because he was the youngest Beatle, we all tended to look on him as the baby. We never let him forget, for instance, that he had been kicked out of Germany for being too young and taunted him with such gibes as 'Still in nappies, weren't you?'

Even some of the fans treated him as a baby. German girls would shout *Liebschen Kind!* (lovely child) at him and he wouldn't mind at all. He always wore a sly grin and had a twinkle in his eyes, perhaps because many of the birds wanted to mother him, which he let them do. Not that he was any kind of 'softie', despite his stature (only Stu had been smaller). He would have a go in a rumpus. And he had a streak of obstinacy which came to the fore now, as he categorically refused to clear up the mess at his bedside.

So the pile of vomit remained. And it began to grow, and grow, mushrooming and taking on a life of its own. Cigarettes were crushed in it, bits of food fed to it, until it assumed the look of a hedgehog; we christened it The Thing. When members of other groups visited us in the flat they took to giving it the occasional drink. Its fame spread and people wanted to come and see it. For a time food and drink seemed to beautify The Thing and it blossomed like a miniature flower garden. It measured something like six inches (15 cm) in diameter. But its beauty was short-lived, and it began to grow hideous. 'I'm frightened to sleep,' George remarked one night, 'in case it eats me.' The Thing began to pong as well, but it was George's baby and somehow we had grown to love it as a pet, despite its wretched origins.

After its fame spread Horst arrived one morning to inspect it. He thought it was a disgusting sight: he was right, of course. He left, returning with a shovel; the end, we knew, was nigh.

'Hey! Don't do that! That's our pet,' we chorused.

Horst was not the sort of man to be put off by mere cries of affection for the squalid Thing. He scooped it up on his shovel and led the way with it out on to the Grosse Freheit while we followed behind him, solemnly chanting the Dead March. The beloved Thing was given a swift burial in a street bin and, only after it had gone to its eternal reward did the cleaner reappear to try to make the flat look fit for human habitation once more. And in the end, it had been something of a minor victory for George: someone else had had to do the dirty work after all.

Lennon was also to make one of his stands of defiance against any sort of authority during our residence in the flat. It was one of those bright May mornings with a clear blue sky, Sunday, and we were almost ready to set out for the Fish Market; a peaceful morning, with people making their way to the Catholic church that stood inexplicably alongside the Star Club in the midst of sex and sin.

Among them were four gentle nuns, who John espied from the flat window as we prepared to leave. 'Going for a pee,' he announced suddenly but instead of going to the bathroom, he went out on to the balcony. There, in full view of whoever might glance upwards, Lennon unzipped and sprinkled the four sisters with a mini-cloudburst out of a cloudless sky. 'Raindrops from heaven!' John gleefully yelled down at the startled nuns, who paused, then walked on serenely, well aware that this was no miracle.

Several people witnessed Lennon's anti-clerical demonstration, amongst them two policemen, whose faces creased into smiles. When we went downstairs into the street a little later they merely handed out a mild rebuke. 'You mustn't do that again, or you'll be sent back to

England,' one told him, scarcely able to stifle his laughter.

The worst that happened to John was a stern verbal caution from club owner Weissleder and Horst Fascher. The Star Club was proud of its reputation as Hamburg's top rock rendezvous and they were wary of it being tarnished by some practical joker with a lack of taste. Scoldings rarely worried John for more than a few minutes. He lived life to his own pattern, doing his own thing, relishing outrageous behaviour as a means of demonstration. Nuns represented the church and the church represented authority and establishment, which he could get along without.

While we were enjoying the freedom of St Pauli, back home in England Brian Epstein had reached a crossroads in his brief life as our manager. There were few more doors left on which to knock in his search to find someone to record us. His family was becoming edgy, concerned that he was wasting his energies on the Beatles when they could be far better deployed in the family business. Desperate, Brian sought parental approval for one more last-ditch assault on London where possibly, he thought, some 'cheapo' minor label might be interested in the Beatles.

His first move after arriving in London was to visit the HMV store in Oxford Street where, he had learned, tapes could be transferred onto disc for a fee of a few pounds. He felt this would make for easier handling and listening. During the course of this operation an engineer showed enough interest in the original songs on the tapes to pass the word on upstairs, where EMI housed its music publishing department. Intrigued by the Beatles, Syd Coleman, the publishing boss, called George Martin's office at Parlophone, the only label in the EMI group which had not already turned us away. The result was an appointment for Eppy to meet Martin, Parlophone's chief, the following day. When he heard our demos, George Martin, who would later confess that he was looking for 'something like a Cliff Richard and the Shadows sound', thought maybe we might fill the bill.

The news came to us in the Grosse Freiheit in a telegram from Brian which George Harrison opened and read out: 'Congratulations boys. EMI request recording session. Please rehearse new material.'

It was another 'morning after the night before', but we managed to smile, then laugh and thump each other on the back by way of celebration. This could be it at long last, one more chance – possibly our last – to crack the Big Time; to show what we could really do. 'Where are we going, lads?' we shouted 'To the toppermost of the poppermost'. Wheels were already beginning to turn in the fertile minds of Lennon and McCartney at the mere mention of 'new material' but there was still a long road to travel. George Martin was only promising to lend an ear, just as Decca had done.

Brian flew out to Hamburg to celebrate this new milestone in the Beatles' chequered history. He spent a whole night crawling round the Hamburg clubs with Lennon on a king-size drinking spree.

'Look at this,' John said triumphantly next day, opening his fist to display 100 marks. 'I got Eppy stoned and while he was crying in his beer I conned him out of a hundred.' It was the kind of thing John could do without ever thinking about it again.

After this we assumed that Brian had returned to Liverpool, but a few days later we saw him emerging from the Roxy on the Reeperbahn, the notorious bar frequented by old queens and transvestites.

'Thought you'd gone home, Brian,' we all said, to which he replied that he had been 'doing business' – but he never did tell us what kind.

Amidst all the revelries on the Grosse Freiheit, during this tour I found myself joining forces with John in writing to a girl back home. Her name was Catherine; I came to know her as Kathy, then Kate, and eventually Kit. She was a regular pop fan, a very keen dancer and followed the rock scene with a friend named Alice, who had a great affection for Paul.

I first met Kathy (she signed the name with a K) during one of our appearances at the Aintree Institute, when I discovered that although she loved the Beatles as a group and the music we made, she was not terribly keen on us as people, taking the view that we were a bunch of big-heads.

We met again at the Cavern, but didn't speak to each other. Then I saw her – still with Alice – at a ten-pin bowling alley which had become a favourite retreat for groups on the Merseyside circuit. I had just finished bowling and, on the spur of the moment, asked her if she fancied a Coke. This time we talked for almost two hours, but not about anything really serious. 'See you,' I said when we parted. That's all.

It was purely a friendly relationship with no dating, until shortly before we left for Hamburg to open the Star Club. Eppy organized a highly successful fan club night at the Cavern, where Kathy had become a protégée of Bob Wooler. She was one of a group of dancers called the King Twisters, put together by Bob to demonstrate the current craze for the Twist to Beatle backing; one of the numbers was my *Peppermint Twist* solo. On fan club night, Bob thought it might be a novel idea if I teamed up with Kathy to twist for the benefit of the members. I wasn't all that keen, I told Bob. 'Why don't you ask her?'

He called her into the bandroom. I agreed to make fool of myself and we went into a quick rehearsal, which only succeeded in creasing Paul up with laughter at my efforts.

'If you can do any better, you get up!' I told him.

Paul went into the twist and it was my turn to laugh. 'Sit down,' I said, 'you'll fall over your feet!'

Thus I found myself partnering the expert Kathy after singing my solo. The crowd loved it and encouraged us with cries of 'keep going!' We must have twisted and twirled for ten minutes in the steaming atmosphere, after which I certainly needed a drink. I thought Kathy might feel like one as well, so I invited her down to the Grapes, that oasis a few yards down Mathew Street. It was the start of a relationship that would make us partners for life. Now, parted from her for seven weeks in the helter-skelter life of Hamburg I realized that I was madly in love with her.

The Beatles

13

THE BOMBSHELL

It was on 6 June 1962, the anniversary of D-Day, that the Beatles, freshly returned from our Hamburg triumph at the Star Club, invaded Number Three Studio at Abbey Road, EMI's celebrated London recording citadel. It would prove to be an historic day for everyone involved – even me, in a way. For the Beatles it was a last-ditch attempt to break into the record business. For George Martin, who probably viewed it initially as just another try-out, it would prove to be a turning point in his life.

George Martin was a gentle man who had been in the Fleet Air Arm during the war. Now, at the age of 36, he was chief of a record label that had attracted most attention – and praise – for its comedy output, guiding the disc destinies of Peter Sellers, the Goons and Peter Ustinov. George, who had studied oboe at the Guildhall School of Music, was also a jazz aficionado and had recorded such stalwarts as Humphrey Lyttelton and Johnny Dankworth. His pop production was small, although, like Bruno Koschmieder and others hungry for talent, he had made several excursions to the Soho coffee bars in the late fifties. He had seen Tommy Steele singing there with the Vipers skiffle group – but signed the Vipers, turning Tommy Steele down, thus leaving the field wide open for Decca very soon afterwards.

Now, a few years later as he gazed upon the Beatles for the first time in Number Three Studio, he noted with some interest that they were clean and tidy, so he has said since. We in turn found him to be a neat, slim, well-spoken type with none of the bounce or swagger or 'Hi-baby' schmaltz of Tin Pan Alley. The other Beatles had a few cheerful exchanges with him but, intent on the task ahead, I quietly got on with setting up my kit so I never entered into any conversation with him.

His extremely professional ear listened intently to a selection of our regular oldies, plus a handful of Lennon-McCartney originals that included the now finalized version of *Love Me Do*, which we had tried out on our Hamburg audiences with much success. Mr Martin, however, showed little apparent excitement afterwards as he talked earnestly with Brian while we packed up our gear. Eppy seemed to be optimistic enough, even though George Martin had not promised anything definite, and we all went home to Liverpool to await the verdict. Again it would be a long time coming.

Life slipped back into the old groove with a memorable seven-till-midnight welcome home at the Cavern on the following Saturday 9 June. We topped the bill that was prominently displayed in a front-page advertisement in *Mersey Beat* which proclaimed that this was our first appearance after our 'success in Germany'. The supporting outfits (in smaller type) were the Red River Jazzmen, Ken Dallas and the Silhouettes and the Four Jays.

Beneath the advertisement and occupying a quarter of the page was a camera study of me in profile with a text that said: 'Congratulations to Pete, Paul, John and George and the boys on their successful engagements in Germany.' It was the first time my name had led the order of Beatles: the usual style had always been John, Paul, George and Pete. However, we had considered ourselves to be a team for so long now, no-one grumbled about it.

After the big Saturday night at the Cavern we trooped off to Manchester once more for a second BBC broadcast. It was another great screaming occasion and on the same bill were the Manchester-based group Freddie and the Dreamers. When the show was over Freddie had a friendly chat with us and was full of wonder about our 'incredible reception'.

Brian saw to it that we were kept extremely busy while he awaited the word from Parlophone. Apart from the Cavern, and dance-hall dates that ranged over a wider geographical area than before, we put in some appearances at the old familiar haunt, the Casbah.

Kathy and I were now dating regularly, although it was impossible to conduct a normal type of courtship. I was drumming nearly every night of the week and Kathy, a shop assistant, was working all day. We had to snatch what little time we could together. We would sometimes catch the 5.30 house at a cinema, then it would be off to work for me.

In Hamburg I had bought her an attractive Japanese-style dress with a slit skirt. So far her family hadn't met me and when I called unexpectedly at her home in the Liverpool suburb of Walton to present it I wondered what kind of reception I might receive. Her brother Richie answered the door and I asked if Kathy was in. 'Are you Pete?' he wanted to know. He went on to tell me she was out dancing, which was no surprise, but he invited me in.

I was introduced to her mother, who looked long and hard at my leather jacket and pants. I knew I was being inspected, but Richie came to my rescue with 'Fancy a pint?'

We spent several hours in the local, where my leathers also attracted considerable attention, and I didn't see Kathy until the following day. But all was well; I had passed the family audition.

It was still only around mid-June when a strange conversation took place in my home during a visit by Joe Flannery, manager of a group called Lee Curtis and the All-Stars and a childhood friend of Epstein's. Out of the blue he said: 'When are you going to join us, Pete?'

I smiled. This was obviously some kind of gag he was pulling. 'You must be joking,' I said. 'Why would I want to quit the Beatles when we're just about to get our big break on Parlophone?'

'Maybe I've jumped the gun,' he said seriously, mumbling something about it obviously being a rumour going the rounds, and we left the subject there.

Why should anyone start a rumour like that? I had no intention of leaving, not after two years as a Beatle, not having travelled this far. But Joe's words nagged at me. Had there been some secret dealing with old pal Epstein? Some talk of switching me or dropping me?

The next weekend we played the Plaza Ballroom at St Helens and at the end of the evening I decided to tackle Brian, repeating the conversation that had taken place with Flannery. Eppy became very quiet, blushed as he always did and started to stammer.

'Look, Brian,' I said, 'are there any plans to replace me in the Beatles?'

'I'm telling you as manager,' he said convincingly, 'there are no plans to replace you, Pete.'

This was good enough for me. The rumour had been quashed for good and all and I thought no more about it as we continued our busy schedule, laughing and clowning, drinking together, travelling together.

There had even been a warning from Brian that my relationship with Kathy 'might be bad for the business'. On the face of it, nothing had changed.

At the end of July, George Martin at last decided to sign the group and record them in September, but, as in the case of the Decca audition, the news was kept from me. John, Paul and George knew the verdict straight away but said absolutely nothing to me, not even a hint. I would learn it the hard way.

Some two weeks after the Parlophone decision, on the night of Wednesday 15 August, we played at the Cavern and, in the normal way, talked later about arrangements for the following night, when we were due to appear at the Riverpark Ballroom in Chester. The regular drill was that Neil Aspinall and I would collect the other Beatles in his van and drive to the venue.

As Lennon was leaving, I called: 'Pick you up tomorrow, John.'

'No,' he said, 'I've got other arrangements.' At the time this didn't strike me as being odd, even though it didn't conform to the usual pattern. John was going through a trying domestic period; in eight days' time he was due to marry Cynthia, who was already pregnant.

Before I left the Cavern that night, Brian told me that he would like to see me the following morning at his office in Whitechapel at 10am. Again there was nothing particularly worrying about this, as we had frequently met there to discuss the business of the Beatles, while my home was still the group headquarters for kit and transport.

Next day Neil drove me into town and dropped me off in Whitechapel. I found Brian in a very uneasy mood when I joined him in his upstairs office. He came out with a lot of pleasantries and talked anything but business, which was unlike him. These were obviously delaying tactics and something important, I knew, was on his mind. Then he mustered enough courage to drop the bombshell.

'The boys want you out and Ringo in...'

I was stunned and found words difficult. Only one echoed through my mind. Why, why, why?

'They don't think you're a good enough drummer, Pete,' Brian went on. 'And George Martin doesn't think you're a good enough drummer.'

'I consider myself as good, if not better, than Ringo,' I could hear myself saying. Then I asked: 'Does Ringo know about this yet?'

'He's joining on Saturday,' Eppy said.

So everything was all neatly packaged. A conspiracy had clearly been going on for some time behind my back, but not one of the other Beatles could find the courage to tell me. The stab in the back had been left to Brian, and it had been left until almost the last minute. Even Ringo had been a party to it, someone else I had considered to be a pal until this momentous day. He and I had kept our friendship rolling whenever possible since that first trip to Hamburg. We would often meet at lunchtime at the Cavern, where musicians tended to congregate whether they were appearing there or not. We would meet at other venues on the same bill and, of course, at my home if Rory Storm was playing the Casbah.

Epstein went on to what for him was simply next business at this shattering meeting. 'There are still a couple of venues left before Ringo joins – will you play?'

'Yes,' I nodded, not really knowing what I was saying, for my mind was in a turmoil. How could this happen to me? Why had it taken two years for John Lennon, Paul McCartney and George Harrison to decide that my drumming was not of a high enough standard for them? Dazed, I made my way out of Brian's office. Downstairs, Neil was waiting for me. 'What's happened?' he asked as soon as he saw me, 'you look as if you've seen a ghost.'

'They've kicked me out!' I said.

Neil could scarcely believe it either. We headed for the Grapes to sink a couple of pints. 'All I want to do is try to get my thoughts together,' I told him. He was really upset and as disgusted as I was at this sudden, stupefying blow. He began to talk about quitting his job as road manager.

'There's no need for that,' I told him. 'Don't be a fool – the Beatles are going places.'

I managed to talk him out of doing anything rash; so he did stay on with the Beatles. One day he would reach his own pinnacle as managing director of the bizarre Apple Corps set up by the Beatles to handle their own affairs. The immediate result, however, was that we would begin to see less of each other and gradually drift apart, even though he was still living in my home. His duties with the Beatles became increasingly demanding after *Love Me Do*'s success and the group was needed farther afield. As 1963 dawned they started touring. Scotland first, then nationwide, and soon Neil, Brian and the Beatles would make London their home. As a result I've had no contact with him for many years.

Once I was home at Hayman's Green, I broke down and wept. My mother already knew what had happened that morning in Brian's office, as unknown to me Neil had slipped away at some stage to telephone her. She had been trying in vain to contact Epstein only to find that he was 'Not available'.

When I was sufficiently recovered from the initial shock, I realized that I had promised to carry on as a Beatle until Ringo's arrival and that we were due to play Chester that night. Now I knew I could never face it. I had been betrayed and sitting up there on stage with the three people who had done it would be like having salt rubbed into a very deep wound. If they didn't want me, they would have to get along without me from this moment on and find another drummer. They must have known that they wouldn't have to roam Liverpool in a desperate search for a replacement; on the same bill at Chester were the Big Three, who would become part of the growing Epstein stable, and in the Big Three there was Johnny Hutch – who two years earlier had sat in as make-do drummer for the Larry Parnes audition.

Neil, still in some torment, carried on with his 'roadie' duties and went off to Chester, where Eppy expressed some surprise and disappointment that I hadn't shown up. 'What did you expect?' was Neil's forthright comment. When he asked John, Paul and George for the real reason for my dismissal he was bluntly told: 'It's got nothing to do with you – you're only the driver...'. Fans who anxiously enquired 'where's Pete Best?' were simply told that I had not been available. Meanwhile I stayed indoors at Hayman's Green for days; numbed, still searching through my mind for a genuine answer to my demise.

My mother managed to get in touch with George Martin, who made it clear that he had never suggested that I must go. All he had said, he explained, was that for the purposes of the Beatles' first record he would rather use a session man. In 1980, George Martin told Patrick Doncaster in an interview for a *Daily Mirror* series: 'Pete certainly seemed to be out of it at the audition. The others laughed and joked and talked among themselves, but he was silent most of the time.

'I never thought that Brian Epstein would let him go. He seemed to be the most saleable commodity as far as looks went, although the rest looked good as well. He had this James Dean image about him.

'It was a surprise when later I learned that they had dropped Pete Best. The drums were important to me for a record, but they didn't matter much otherwise. Fans don't pay particular attention to the quality of drumming.'

When the Beatles arrived at Abbey Road with their new drummer Ringo Starr, George Martin wasn't going to chance using him on sight, either, and brought in instead a seasoned session man named Andy White. Ringo, however, sat in on some of the takes. George Martin said: 'We finished up with several versions of *Love Me Do*, using both Ringo and Andy White. I honestly can't remember which side was issued, but I feel it was one with Ringo on it. On the versions with Andy I had Ringo playing tambourine.'

Mersey Beat blasted the news of my dismissal – although they didn't call it that – in an exclusive, headlined: BEATLES CHANGE DRUMMER! The issue was dated 23 August – the day that Lennon married Cyn. The story began: 'Ringo Starr (former drummer with Rory Storm and the Hurricanes) has joined the Beatles, replacing Pete Best on drums. Ringo has admired the Beatles for years and is delighted with the new arrangement. Naturally he is tremendously excited about the future.

'The Beatles comment: "Pete left the group by mutual agreement. There were no arguments or difficulties, and this has been an entirely amicable decision..."'

No Beatle was named, and the only mutual agreement had been between John, Paul and George. There were no arguments because not one of them had had the nerve to discuss the decision with me and there were no difficulties because my firing had been a *fait accompli* with Ringo already hired. And, of course, I hadn't 'left' the group: I had been booted out.

That John Lennon had not even dared to face me bit deeply. I was closer to him than I was to any other Beatle; I had known him intimately for around four years, which is a long time in a young life and I was fond of him and had much respect for him.

In the Beatles' authorized biography published in 1968, author Hunter Davies writes: 'The sacking of Pete Best is one of the few murky incidents in the Beatles' history. There was something sneaky the way it was done. Admittedly, most people would have done the same and got the manager to do the dirty work. But all of them, especially John, had always been so honest and truthful with everyone...'. John told Davies: 'We were cowards when we sacked him. We made Brian do it. But if we'd told Pete to his face, that would have been much nastier than getting Brian to do it. It would probably have ended in a fight if we'd told him...'

What would have been so terrible about that? At least I would have had the opportunity to defend myself, to answer my criticism and probably plead my case before we came to blows. It would have been our first fight. Over the years John and I had several arguments, usually about the material we were playing, arrangements, perhaps the running order – the usual trivial problems that occur frequently in the life of a group. But we never fought or fell out.

There had been a strong bond between us and when we regularly began to play at the Cavern he would sometimes sleep at my home. We would arrive there late after the Casbah had closed for the night and descend into the deserted coffee bar, wolfing back bags of crisps and sinking dozens of bottles of Coke. 'We'll leave the money on the bar,' we would tell Mo. Neither of us ever did and mother would never chase us for it.

Then there would be the regular sewing sessions after John had ripped his pants during his frenzied leaps on stage. 'Mo,' he would say, 'it's a needle and thread job. Split me jeans again and I've got to be ready to go out in the morning.' He would sometimes carry out the running repairs himself on her electric sewing machine, which he had taken the trouble to learn to use.

We would rise about eleven in the morning to be at the Cavern by midday, refreshed by a whacking breakfast. John could go through a whole loaf of bread with dripping and bacon, but sometimes the menu would simply consist of toast and Coke. Before setting out, we would always find time to spin a few records. This was the John I knew; but his action with the other Beatles meant the end of a never-to-be-forgotten friendship.

The brief news that the Beatles had simply changed drummers soon had its repercussions. A stream of fans started to call at my door in Hayman's Green, weeping girls who wanted to know why I had left the group; girls who became extremely angry when they were told that I had been dismissed. Mo remembers her living room 'bulging with fans, sighing and sobbing'.

Several girls, almost heartbroken it seemed, did not want to leave me and showed their devotion by keeping vigil outside my home, even sleeping out through the night in the garden.

As the real story spread there was violent reaction at the Cavern with near riots and demonstrations outside Eppy's Whitechapel base. Fans

R

marched, paraded, picketed and yelled with such fervour that the popular Mr Epstein found himself one of the most disliked characters in Liverpool. The jostling protesters were enough to scare him away from appearing anywhere near the Cavern with the Beatles.

After a couple of days of absence however they decided to venture forth, but only after club owner Ray McFall provided Epstein with a bodyguard. The throng were waiting with their chants and banners which read PETE FOR EVER, RINGO NEVER!, PETE IS BEST! and WE WANT PETE! They were waiting to scratch and claw and maul Eppy and the new-style Beatles. Fists flew, hair was pulled and in the mêlée George Harrison received a black eye – which was still visible when they recorded *Love Me Do* in September.

Some fans were convinced that the Beatles could never survive without me perched there behind the drums and they were prepared to try to tear out Ringo's hair to drive home their point. 'Pete *was* the Beatles' was a familiar cry from my supporters, who also went into action against pro-John, Paul and George devotees. *Mersey Beat* received petitions signed by hundreds of people demanding my reinstatement. Ringo found himself on the receiving end of poison-pen letters, some of which contained threats. Nevertheless, he shaved off his beard and combed his hair forward; he was in and I was out and the decision would be final, despite what the loyal fans thought.

Mo received a constant stream of visitors wanting to make it clear that they had in no way been involved. First was Bob Wooler. Then came Rory Storm, who considered that Ringo had left him in the lurch during a Butlin's summer season. Rory's mother called, too.

During August, George Harrison forgot about his bruised eye long enough to write to a fan named Jenny: 'Ringo is a much better drummer, and he can smile – which is a bit more than Pete could do. It will seem different for a few weeks, but I think that the majority of our fans will soon be taking Ringo for granted ... lots of love from George.' (This letter, along with other Beatles memorabilia, was auctioned at Sotheby's in London just before Christmas, 1981.)

During the week after my eclipse the Granada Company were televising the new Beatles from the Cavern and Neil Aspinall wondered if I might have recovered enough by now to go along. I thought a lot about having to face people and a stream of embarrassing questions but decided that I would look in.

That's what it amounted to when the time came. I sneaked in and sneaked out again, knowing that it would all be too much to bear. On the way out Paul's father Jim noticed me and said jubilantly, 'Great, isn't it? They're on TV!', which didn't seem terribly tactful.

'Sorry, Mr McCartney,' I said, 'I'm not the right person to ask...'

Meanwhile, Epstein had finally been in touch with my mother and

Previous page: Rory Storm and the Hurricanes, featuring Ringo Starr on drums.
Inset: Now clean-shaven, Ringo replaces Pete as the Beatles' drummer.

had told her that he would like to see me, 'as a personal favour,' he added. So we met again. He was anxious to retain my friendship, he said, and was profuse in his apologies about what had happened. 'I didn't want to lose you from the group,' he impressed on me. 'It was the pressure from the rest of them.'

'Let's get it out into the open, Brian,' I told him. 'None of them was man enough to tell me and left you to do the dirty work.'

It was a duty as manager that he hadn't relished, he admitted, and he had spent a sleepless night before facing me on that fateful morning. Then he tried to be more cheerful and said: 'I have an idea that might work. I'm thinking of signing the Mersey Beats and I'd like you to join them.'

The Mersey Beats were a young outfit that were attracting some attention with their Beatle-based approach.

'I can't do that,' I told Brian. 'I've been in the number one stall in the stable and now you want me to join an up-and-coming group. It just won't work. If I'm going to join another group it will have to be a clean break.'

After more apologies from Eppy we shook hands. This was goodbye; but I did wonder why my so-called 'suspect' drumming was good enough for the Mersey Beats, when it hadn't been for the Beatles only a week or two before.

Offers began to come my way to enrol in other groups from managers who saw the potential of having me on drums, but none of them really attracted me. Then Joe Flannery came round to Hayman's Green once more, inviting me to join Lee Curtis and the All-Stars. This did sound a better prospect, although I asked Joe to give me time to consider the proposal. After two days of careful thought I decided to bid for stardom with Lee Curtis and Joe returned to my home again. This time I took the opportunity of recalling his much earlier visit. 'It puzzles me how you were able to let the cat out of the bag so long ago,' I said. 'How did you know?'

Joe confessed that he had heard a whisper 'on the grapevine', but that was as far as he would go. He insisted he wasn't in a position to reveal the details. But I had heard stories on the grapevine as well which hinted that he had the word from his old friend Eppy, but I never did discover if this really was the truth. I made my first appearance with the All-Stars on Monday 10 September at the Majestic Ballroom in Birkenhead, where the warmth of the fantastic welcome helped to set me on the road back. On the following day in London the Beatles recorded *Love Me Do*.

In spite of my new position in the All-Stars I could never forget that I was a Beatle and the reasons for my dismissal plagued me when I was alone with my thoughts. So I was 'sullen', 'didn't smile enough' and, I later found out from reading Epstein's own book, 'too conventional to be a Beatle and though friendly with John, he was not with George and Paul'. Other people on the beat scene were convinced that I had been sacked because I refused to change my hairstyle.

Since 15 August 1962 I have never had any conversation with John, Paul or George and thus have never received any satisfactory explanation. Never to my face, during my two years as a Beatle, did one of them declare that my drumming was not up to standard (it had met with Bert Kaempfert's approval) or implored me to cultivate a fringe. Right to the end we were still drinking together and seemingly the best of friends.

My mother is convinced to this day that the real reason was jealousy and that we had reached the point where people were referring to us as 'Pete Best and the Beatles'. If it was true that I had become the star of the group then it was something that evolved and not a position I had striven for. Bob Wooler's early tag of 'mean and moody' caught on and was a useful catchphrase, but I never considered myself to be a Beatles' king-pin. Everyone of us endured his share of mobbing and I never tried to analyse fan reaction enough to determine if one of us was receiving more attention than the other.

I admit that some of the adulation that came my way could have caused some jealousy, though I was never aware of it. As early as January 1961, at the Aintree Institute, fans presented me with a giant Teddy Bear. There was nothing for John, Paul or George and I have the gift to this day, still wrapped in its original Polythene.

Bill Harry, in his introduction to *Mersey Beat: The Beginnings of the Beatles*, a collection of pages from the paper published in book form in 1977, wrote that I was 'the most popular Beatle as far as the Liverpool girl fans were concerned', but that in the early days he had found me somewhat withdrawn, like Stuart Sutcliffe. He also described me as 'a figure with mystique, darkly good-looking and seemingly the one most likely to emerge as the most popular Beatle'.

However, I was not even in the front line of the act. True, Bob Wooler sometimes insisted on moving me forward with my drums, but everybody had his own spot in the Beatles and this could not have been a danger signal to the rest. Occasionally my popularity did seem to surpass theirs, I suppose, but we were still a team and I really wasn't getting any different treatment. It was Brian Epstein who made it a rule that I 'must get up and do a number'. *Peppermint Twist* became an essential part of the Beatles' presentation and was always much appreciated, but it didn't make me *the* star. Paul would equally have the girls drooling with his ballads.

Maybe there could have been some discussion among them of the possibility that I could at some stage overshadow them. The *Mersey Beat* listing of my name first on the front page would not have helped if this were the case. In addition, it is possible that when I acted as manager before Eppy arrived on the scene, I attracted more attention in the business field. This was natural, by virtue of the circumstances, but the three of them left this side to me without complaint.

My attitude always was that we were all popular and as long as the group was being acclaimed there was no problem. Perhaps I should have read some kind of danger signal into being mobbed while sometimes they stood on the sideline, but this again never occurred to me. I certainly had no idea that I was so popular until the break came. The reaction was unbelievable and only then did I realize how many real fans I had.

As for the criticism that I was shy, this was probably due to the fact that, deeply involved in my drumming, I used to keep my head down, looking at the skins. Perhaps that is why George Martin concluded that I was sullen. However this just didn't make sense. You didn't get 'shy, sullen' lads leap-frogging down the Reeperbahn, taking on anyone in a scrap or playing the large field I had played in pursuit of the opposite sex.

Oddly, nearly a year after Ringo had taken my place at the drums, John Lennon was sufficiently worried to say in a 'message to Merseyside' printed in *Mersey Beat* on 18 July, 1963: 'I would also like to point out to the people who say that Ringo is always kept in the background – this is not deliberate. Paul, George and I think Ringo is gear and have been trying to bring him forward in the act. However, Ringo is still rather shy and it will take a bit of time. In six months Ringo will really be playing a major part in the act.'

On the night of my twenty-first birthday on 24 November 1962 I was drumming at the Majestic Ballroom in Birkenhead once more. Bob Wooler, as ever the compere, announced this milestone while fans trekked to the stage with presents for me. Bob read out two greetings telegrams. The first was from Joe Flannery and the boys. 'The second,' Bob told the audience, 'is rather special. "Congratulations, many happy returns, all the best – John, Paul, George, Ringo and Brian"'.

I saw the Beatles by chance only two or three times after the split. We never acknowledged each other or exchanged a word. The first occasion was the Granada TV session at the Cavern (this was repeated on ITV on New Year's Day, 1984, including the cry from a Best fan of 'We want Pete!'). The second was when the Lee Curtis outfit were on the same bill as the Beatles at the Cavern. The last was at the Majestic Ballroom, this time for a *Mersey Beat* poll-winners' concert after the All-Stars had come second to the Beatles; they were to follow us on the bill. As I came off stage and they went on we just walked past each other.

I advertised my mother-of-pearl drum kit for sale in a local newspaper, giving only my telephone number. When a young lad arrived to look them over I kept the bass skin with the glorious sunset on it to the rear, thinking that perhaps it would devalue the merchandise. 'Yeah!' he said excitedly when he turned the drum round, his face lighting up, 'I'll have 'em!' He paid the £45 I had asked without a murmur, and the last link had been severed.

GREETINGS T LEGRAM

A/116 GTG 6.1 . LIVERPOOL T 21

GREETINGS PETE BEST
MAJESTIC BALLROOM
CONWAY STREET
BIRKENHEAD =

CONGRATULATIONS MANY HAPPY RETURNS

ALL THE BEST =

JOHN PAUL GEORGE RINGO AND BRIAN +

GPO

Pete's twenty-first birthday greetings telegram from the Beatles and Brian Epstein.

14

I LIVE TO FIGHT ANOTHER DAY

It was like starting life all over again. I had to try to push aside the ever-recurring thoughts that I had been a Beatle for two years; instead I wanted to challenge them in the pursuit of fame as a Lee Curtis All-Star. There was still time, it seemed.

My ex-colleagues did not enjoy an overnight breakthrough, when *Love Me Do* was released at the beginning of October. There was no sudden explosion into the charts, even though the faithful on Merseyside bought it in their hundreds. The record progressed slowly, with little early acclaim from the disc jockeys, creeping first into the lower echelon of the Top Fifty, then the Thirty and finally the Twenty, coming to a halt at number seventeen shortly before Christmas, 1962. Of course, it was certainly an achievement to find a niche in the national lists with a first record, but for me it meant that perhaps there was breathing space yet.

I settled down with the All-Stars, playing the old familiar haunts, and still attracting a loyal following. After I had made a call to Horst Fascher, we took the well-worn trail to Hamburg to appear at the Star Club, and we notched up a successful tour that gave me some heart.

I didn't find the atmosphere in Hamburg any different from my old Beatle days. The Lee Curtis All-Stars were accepted very well by the German audiences and Hamburg itself was still the great merry-go-round it had long been. I saw Astrid once during this trip, still a sad lady who would never forget the happiness she had found with Stu. She made no direct mention of my split with the Beatles; she simply asked me if I had seen any of them. When I said no, she said, 'I'm sorry it happened,' in her nice, sweet way.

My own romance with Kathy was stronger than ever. She had stood by me when the break came and helped me face the music. She was there at Hayman's Green with my family and all our friends when I arrived home from Hamburg. At the right moment I called her into the front room so we could be alone for a few minutes. 'I've got something to tell you,' I said and from the worried look on her face I think she feared that it might be bad news – possibly even the end of our relationship. But I put her mind at rest by pulling a little velvet-lined case from my pocket, opening it to reveal two gold Continental-style engagement rings I had bought in Germany, one for each of us. I slipped one on Kathy's finger and the other on mine. 'We've just got engaged!' I explained to her. There were smiles, embraces and a kiss.

When Mo joined us a little later I announced the great news. 'Well!' she said to Kathy, 'what a surprise – congratulations! He never told me anything about it – did you know?' Kathy had to confess that our engagement was also a complete surprise to her.

We were married in August, 1963, by which time the Beatles were exploding right across the country. *Please, Please Me*, released in January, became their first Number One within a month. It was followed by *From Me To You*, which came out in April, along with their first album – which would top the LP charts for six months. In the August of my marriage came *She Loves You*, and the 'yeh-yeh-yehs' would begin to echo through the world. The Beatles were everywhere.

Meanwhile, after a year of getting nowhere, I split with Lee Curtis and Joe Flannery. Lee had been signed to a solo recording contract, leaving the All-Stars high and dry at a time when, in the wake of the Beatles, the disc companies were signing anything that walked in Liverpool.

Joe had not enhanced my career one bit. The crunch came when Lee was booked to appear in a TV spectacular featuring several groups from the growing Epstein stable which were not yet big names. Again the All-Stars were left out in the cold, which led to a lot of ill-feeling. Time was now valuable in the race to fame and the boys, disenchanted and deserted, asked me to look after them, so we became the Pete Best All-Stars.

The Pete Best All-Stars consisted of myself, Tony Waddington and Wayne Bickerton, who wrote original songs for us, and a lad named Frank Bowen, who didn't stay long and was replaced by Tommy McGurk. We would become the Pete Best Four and eventually, when Tommy quit, the Pete Best Combo.

With the formation of the Pete Best All-Stars, we acquired a new manager, someone who was and still is very close to me, my mother. The Casbah closed in October, 1963 and from then on she worked ceaselessly for me, but it was going to be a rough ride. If we were going to pursue the Beatles we would need a lot of breaks and already it looked like an almost impossible task.

Mo, a lady with immense drive and passion, travelled to London with our tapes, where she found ready listeners at Decca in Dick Rowe and Mike Smith, to whom I was no stranger. In June 1964 they launched us as the Pete Best Four with a single entitled *I'm Gonna Knock On Your*

Door. Mo continued to knock on doors on our behalf, bombarding the press with information and setting up interviews with columnists (a *Daily Mirror* column was headed 'Mum helps an ex-Beatle to try again'); it seemed that the wheels were beginning to turn again, even if slowly.

Ironically, as our disc came out another track on which I had played drums showed up in the charts: John Lennon's solo effort, *Ain't She Sweet*, which we made for Bert Kaempfert in Hamburg three years earlier. Unfortunately, *I'm Gonna Knock On Your Door* failed to make an entry and some of my earlier enthusiasm dimmed as the weeks went by.

We were now beginning to come up against what I called the invisible shield, an all-pervasive force that seemed to say 'So far and no farther!' It was as though the Beatles had stitched a web across all my entrances to the Big Time. This barrier was something I felt very strongly. I couldn't reach out and touch it, but it was there all right. It began some 60 miles outside Liverpool, which was as far away as promoters would book us. Trying to break into London was like trying to go to the moon. Then even Liverpool began gradually to close in on us as the invisible shield moved nearer and nearer.

As a Beatle I had been overwhelmed with fan worship and friendship. It had always been 'Good old Pete', but the magic slowly began to fade after I was kicked out. When the Beatles found fame, the interest in me wore even thinner. It was an almost imperceptible process, like a dripping tap relentlessly working on a stone.

Promoters and bookers crossed our names off their lists. When we failed to knock on enough doors with our single, Decca shelved us along with the rest of the material we had recorded for them. The Beatles themselves certainly never held out a helping hand and only contributed to the destruction with their readily-printed gossip that I had never really been a Beatle, that I didn't smile, that I was unsociable and definitely not a good mixer. There was not a single friendly word from any one of them. Magazines both in Britain and across the Atlantic had been printing far-fetched stories that I had quit the Beatles because of illness and that Ringo was called in only because I was too sick to play. By 1965 these stories would reach a peak of vindictiveness. Even Bob Wooler, who had earlier been enthralled by my 'mean moody magnificence', lost interest in me.

As the Beatles strode on, conquering the world, sitting astride the charts everywhere, my group was going through a hard time. There was little or no revenue coming in, barely enough to pay my bills, and I reached the stage where I found myself scratching around for enough money to buy a packet of cigarettes. I just couldn't sit back and ignore the fact that I should have shared in the Beatles' success, which I considered to be part of my heritage. In the depths of depression I

Pete at the drums with the Pete Best Four.

PETER BEST
Formerly of the
BEATLES
SINGS
Boys
AND
Kansas City
cameo
C- 391

veral albums and singles were released – itimately and otherwise – in the name of Pete Peter) Best. Record companies in Europe and erica were quick to cash in on Pete's former atles connection, with varying success. One lian album featuring Pete with Lonnie megan was produced completely without rmission, from unmixed tracks from a shelved sion, while others re-packaged existing tracks. se include a US album titled 'The Beatle That ne Forgot' and a rare Greek release called surrection – Rebirth of Pete Best, Ex-Beatle'.

decided to take my life, a secret I have kept closely until now.

Kathy and I had started a family by this time and were living in three rooms in the family home at Hayman's Green, a sort of self-contained suite on the first floor, which gave us privacy. On the fateful night the world closed in on me Kathy was away visiting her mother. Methodically I prepared for my exit, locking our bedroom door and blocking the gap beneath it with a towel to prevent the air from coming in. I shut the window, then placed a pillow in front of the old-fashioned gas fire, turned on the jets and lay down my head to await the end.

I was in a semi-coma when I heard vague sounds at the door, but too drowsy to appreciate what was going on. The towel had not been enough to prevent the fumes from seeping through to the wide landing outside, and my brother Rory smelled them as he was passing. He began to wrench at the door handle, but when he found that the door had been locked he battered it down in a frenzy of kicks and, almost choking on the fumes himself, dragged me on to the landing and opened every window in sight.

He called Mo and together they worked for several hours to revive me. They walked me up and down endlessly, halting only to fill me with cup after cup of strong coffee, encouraging me all the time with soothing words until I began to return to the land of the living.

Once I had become stabilized their mood changed a little. Rory told me that I was 'a bloody idiot'. My mother had been frightened by my attempt on my life but now she was annoyed with me, rightly accusing me of being stupid for letting the Beatles' success get me down. She felt I was taking the coward's way out.

I began to feel terribly ashamed. I had let myself and my family down. Not only did Mo admonish me, she threatened to tell Kathy what I had done on her return. 'No,' I insisted, 'that's something I must do myself.'

Next day I confessed the whole episode; my wife was both shocked and upset that I had sought escape in death. 'After all we've been through,' she said. 'We've got to stick together.'

I promised her nothing like it would never happen again. Just as importantly, I promised myself the same thing. When I fully recovered I vowed that I would buckle down and give showbusiness one more try.

The Pete Best Four took to the road again, but still found that invisible shield barring our way to success. By this time groups were saturating the scene, all trying to scale the heights reached by the Beatles, but most of them would fall by the wayside.

During 1965 one door suddenly opened to us – a North American tour with most venues in Canada. It would be a tour to promote an album we would record in New York for an independent company, the Mr Maestro label, headed by an American record executive named Dave Rolnick. Tommy McGurk left us when the tour came up and with the addition of two saxes we would become the Pete Best Combo.

It was thrilling news and I saw it as a make-or-break chance for me, an opportunity to crack that barrier. It wasn't going to be a great barn-storming tour making the world's front pages or even those in North America – the Beatles and Rolling Stones were doing that – but we flew off in high spirits across the Atlantic and some of the old excitement began to flow again.

We cut a dozen tracks for a Mr Maestro album with the catchy title of *Best of the Beatles*. Featured on it were six standards and six Combo originals conjured up by Tony Waddington and Wayne Bickerton. The label also put us out on singles.

On the promotion tour we received a fantastic welcome at every stop and played to packed houses. I was amazed by the warmth of it all. Again there was the clamour of new-found fans, the scramble for autographs, the shrill screams. But as the early weeks went past there was no sign of the Pete Best Combo making a dent in the North American charts. Nevertheless I caused a sensation when in September the news leaked out that I was suing Brian Epstein and the Beatles for breach of contract, and Ringo Starr for libel.

The legal proceedings concerning breach of contract had been set in motion in 1963, when I had engaged a Liverpool lawyer to act for me. They were still going on when the American tour was offered. Meanwhile, in February, 1965, an astonishing interview with the Beatles appeared in *Playboy*, the internationally famous American men's magazine. John Lennon was quoted as saying: ...'Ringo used to fill in sometimes if our drummer was ill. With his periodic illness.' Then Ringo came in with: 'He took little pills to make him ill.' The implication obviously was that I had been some kind of a drug addict. It was a lie that would be picked up by other publications and fan magazines.

Of course I was astounded and hurt by the personal slur attributed to Ringo. I had known him since the early Casbah days, had become closer when we were in Hamburg together and really reckoned him to be a mate when our paths crossed at the Cavern while he was with Rory Storm. We would talk drums together, drink together and I would have no reason to doubt that he was anything but a friend. Suddenly in print, he was 'going gangster' on me.

On the advice of my Liverpool lawyer I engaged two United States attorneys to act for me during the American tour. When the news broke while we were there it was reported in some American papers and in the *Daily Mirror* in London that I was claiming more than £15 million from the Beatles 'and others' in separate actions, but this was an exaggerated figure announced by Dave Rolnick purely as a publicity boost for the tour.

Legal wrangling would drag on for some four years on both sides of

Ludwig
BUY THE
BOND
CRITERION
PICTURE OF THE

BOND'S
America's Largest Clothier

the Atlantic. Eventually both actions would be bracketed together in an out-of-court settlement and the resulting damages could never have been described as being substantial. Epstein, remember, had never signed the original contract.

Money, however, had not been my main concern when I sued for libel. I worried more about this attack on my character and derived most satisfaction from the fact that I had been cleared. However, accusations such as this have a habit of sticking.

The Pete Best Combo's North American tour lasted six months and only came to an end because of the strict man-for-man exchange system that existed between the Musicians Unions in Britain and the United States. According to union rules, I could have remained, but the rest of the boys would have to go home. I couldn't desert them, so we all packed our bags for Liverpool.

Once there, it was back to the old routine, plodding along as one amongst dozens of groups, the chances of hitting the jackpot diminishing daily. In the end we had to face the truth that there was no future for the group. Two of the boys had decided to become married men and we all called it a day. Another era had passed.

In 1968 I said goodbye to showbusiness and, with the responsibility of a wife and two daughters to support, had reached one more crossroads in life. It took a lot of soul-searching before making the break, along with a succession of restless nights. Financially, the position was not good and for the first time I had to find a job that didn't involve sitting behind a drum kit.

In those days there were jobs to be had, but whenever I told a prospective employer that I had only worked in showbusiness there was always the suspicion that I would simply fill a post until something else beckoned me back for another stab at the bright lights. I had to prove to people that I was willing to work, to devote my energies to a job and stick to it.

I did shift work as a labourer in a twenty-four hour bakery; I sliced bread and suffered 'Baker's sting', an occupational hazard resulting from getting your fingers mixed up with the slicing saw. My days as a Beatle now seemed like a distant dream. This was the real world; to prove myself I toiled on as a baker's man until 1969, when the Civil Service threw me a lifeline with the offer of a position in the employment service. I grabbed it.

I have been a civil servant ever since, with just a few excursions into showbusiness. The first, in 1978, was brief. Dick Clark, the American TV pop personality and producer, invited me over to Los Angeles to appear in a nostalgic spectacular featuring veterans of the rock scene. While I was there, surprise, surprise, my phone rang one day, and an old familiar voice came on the other end of the line. It was Tony Sheridan,

Previous page: The Pete Best Combo on tour in America. Insets: back in England.

who was resident in the San Fernando Valley. We had a glorious reunion and recalled the epic two hour scrap we had in Hamburg in the early sixties.

In 1979 Dick Clark acted as executive producer to a remarkable documentary-style movie called *The Birth of the Beatles* which featured lookalikes playing the main roles. He called me in to be technical adviser, and as the Civil Service granted me leave of absence, I visited the States once more to help promote the film. There were plans that I might work and settle there, but the necessary visa was never forthcoming, so it was back to the Civil Service where, happily, I remain, although I have crossed the Atlantic a couple of times since to appear in 'Where Are They Now?' programmes.

I have my own home in West Derby, not far from my mother and the long-gone Casbah Club. For many years my two daughters, Beba and Bonita, now in their teens, never knew that I had once been a Beatle. It would have meant nothing to them during their early years, anyway, and it was only at school later that the other kids started to ask them if it was true that their dad was Pete Best, the Beatle. I had to admit that I was.

It is a part of my life that will always be with me, particularly the memory of the way I was axed just as the Beatles were about to hit the biggest time ever.

All the memories of the good and bad times we had shared as Beatles came flooding back early that December morning in 1980 when the news of John Lennon's assassination filled the radio bulletins. I was stunned and saddened. It was all over for John, my one-time friend. I remembered how he could sometimes be so loving, warm and tender but at others just an out-and-out bastard. I remember how he could also be withdrawn. He was seldom forthcoming about his background or family, although he frequently moaned about Aunt Mimi who, according to him, was for ever criticizing and scolding because of his manner of dress and conduct in general. But he would never open up completely about the father he hadn't seen since early childhood, or his mother, who had been killed in a road accident in 1958.

I only met Aunt Mimi on two occasions and she didn't seem to be very much impressed with either of us. Once, en route to a venue, we stopped off at her home to collect a guitar.

'You're going to meet Mimi now,' he warned me. 'She's very straight-laced. Just say yes or no, nice day, isn't it? Don't get involved. She's always dressing me down in front of people and she'll say things like "Look at the state of him! Hair down his neck! Cowboy boots!"' I took his word for it.

I managed to muster a glimpse of a smile on the day he died as I remember him playing his favourite trick – pretending to be blind at a zebra crossing or traffic lights somewhere in Liverpool's busy city centre.

The rest of the Beatles, or a policeman if one was near, would make sure that the flow of vans, cars and buses had halted and then John would meander slowly across the street until around the halfway mark. There he would stick his tongue out or wink at drivers or the cop – then he'd beat it.

I pictured the drunken John, when he could be either extremely amusing or viciously tempered, raging at the nearest victim he could find, fans included. They were 'hunch-backed Quasimodos', 'gits' or 'spastics' or maybe 'four-eyed bastards'. Sober the following day he would claim he didn't remember blowing his top. 'God! Did I say that?' he would blink in disbelief. But there was never any remorse.

Once a fan stuck his head round the bandroom door at the Cavern, a big friendly smile on his face, only to be greeted with a ferocious roar from John. 'Get out! Get knotted before I give you the boot!'

He found a butt in one devoted Cavern fan named Bernie, who would do anything for us like a willing slave, fetching and carrying, even volunteering to hump our kit. Day after day he would be ragged by John yet still come back for more. Often Lennon would gruffly dispatch him to the Grapes to have our pints ready and waiting on arrival, and as soon as the glasses needed replenishing Bernie would be called on to do his duty again.

I recalled once more that even from the early days John had made it quite clear that he would get to the top – no matter who he had to tread on. 'One day – by one means or another,' he said more than once, 'we'll have a record in the charts. If we have to be bent or con people, then that's what we'll have to do to get there.

'It doesn't matter what it takes to get to the top. It might cause some heartache, but once I'm up there it'll be a different kettle of fish.' Yes, he did say '*I*' and not '*we*'. That was the real John Lennon, brilliant, amusing but ruthless.

Meantime I am still getting some harassment from the country that Lennon made his own. The libels and slanders still go on and a lot of unkind and uncharitable stories still find their way into print, mostly in American magazines. According to a recent one I have been in an American jail for five years on 'a heroin bust'. I have also been reported dead and been described as having been terribly disfigured in a car crash – but I suppose the lunatic fringe of the press always has to find something more outrageous to say.

Beatles pilgrims, fan club members from many parts of the world, but particularly from America and Japan, still turn up at Hayman's Green hoping to see the Casbah. My mother talks to many of them and the frequent question they ask of her is: 'Does Pete still have any regrets?'

She tells them that my sacking caused me a lot of heartache and grief at the time and adds: 'It's like a cut – it bleeds, it heals, but the scar's still there...'

Which just about sums it up.

The poster designed for the Casbah Club by Paul McCartney's brother Mike – otherwise known as Mike McGear of the Scaffold.

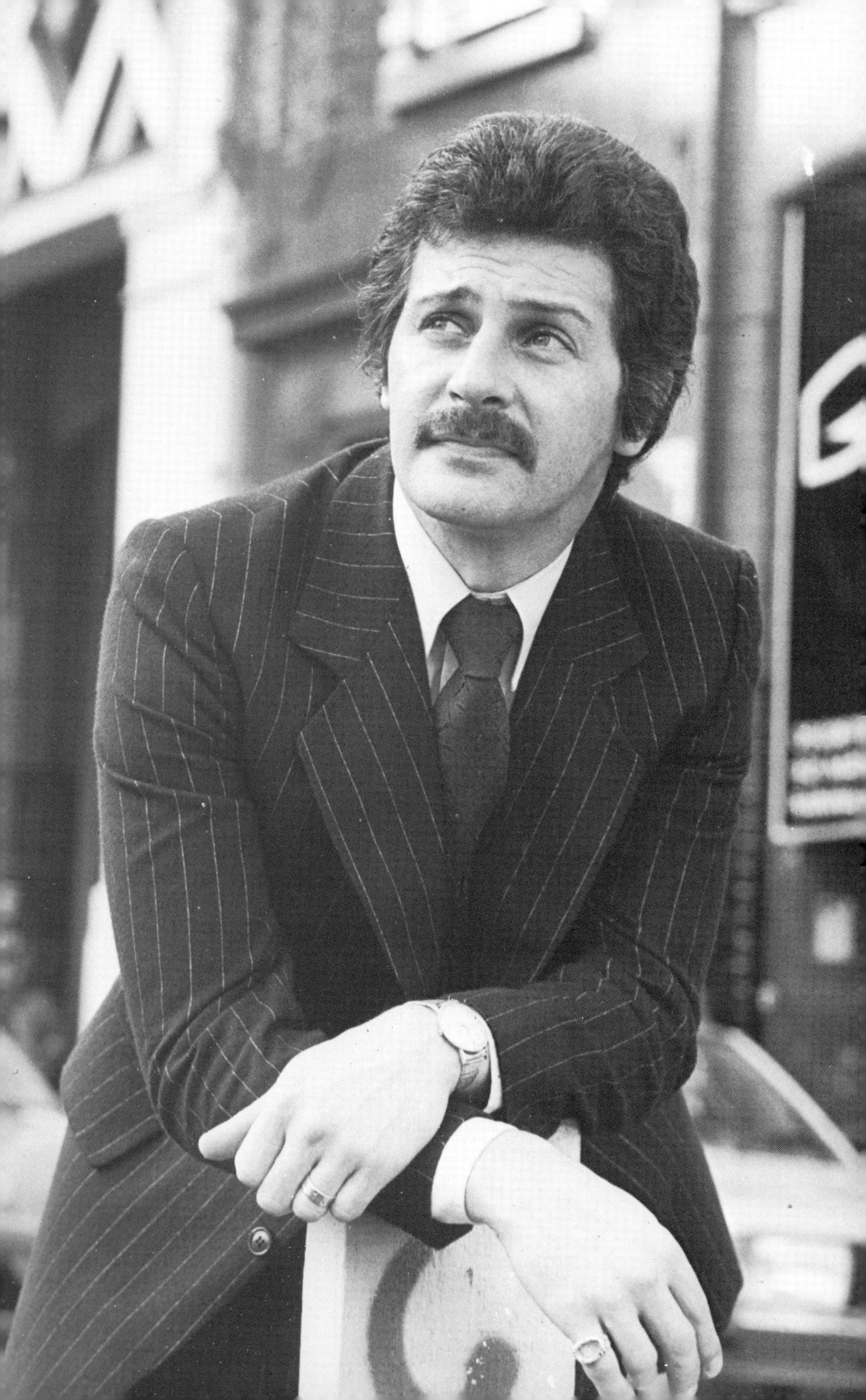

15

DOWN AMONG THE GHOSTS

Today my mother uses the basement that was the Casbah as a store place and my youngest brother Roag, who has a group called the Watt Four, practises his drumming in what was the coffee bar.

On the wall above the fireplace there is a permanent reminder of the great days: a copy of one of the earliest Beatles posters which I etched in silver on black. The original was designed by Paul's brother Mike McCartney and shows a stomping guitarist in silhouette. The figure is of George Harrison, in typical stance, hair standing up in spikes.

Sometimes I wander down to my old home and let my mind take a stroll. Even as I walk up the drive at Number Eight Hayman's Green the clock seems to turn back and I hear the sounds of laughter and the beat of the old thriving days.

Down in the basement the memories come flooding in and I recall the faces of the musicians and of the staunch members and I hear the tinkle of the shillings in the cash box.

I go back to my schooldays, when I used to hurry through my homework in time to stock up the Cokes and be ready for the excitement of 7.30, when a record would blare forth on the jukebox signalling that the Casbah was about to open its doors. I picture my other brother Rory, who was about fourteen or so at the time, greasing his hair beforehand to try to cut something of a dash as he served at the coffee bar. Then in would pour the crowd.

So much happened down there beneath my home; I think of all the hard work that went into making the Casbah and I steal a quick glance at the black ceiling hiding John Lennon's potbellied caricatures. I imagine once more the cavalcade of motorbikes arriving; the girls queueing outside; the lads coming in from the pubs around ten to find themselves under the scrutiny of Frank Garner, a lovely, genial character who was a judo black belt and could deal with any objectionable scousers.

Alone in the Casbah I sometimes play Roag's drums and close my eyes to recapture the atmosphere.

Absent or former friends are there in my memories: Stu Sutcliffe, Lennon, Eppy (who was to die accidently at the age of 32 at his London home in 1967 from 'incautious overdoses' of sleeping pills, as the inquest concluded). And Rory Storm, who was to die five years later of a drug overdose in what appeared to be a suicide pact with his mother at their Liverpool home.

I lay aside the drumsticks and the music and the laughter and the memories are lost in a cloud. It wouldn't take very long to clear the Casbah and restore it to its former glory. But it could never be the same...